KNOXVILLE HISTORY PROJECT presents

Historic KNOXVILLE

THE *Curious* VISITOR'S GUIDE TO ITS *Stories* AND *Places*

RESEARCHED & WRITTEN BY
JACK NEELY

EDITED & IMAGES SOURCED BY
PAUL JAMES

RESEARCHED & WRITTEN BY
Jack Neely

EDITED, IMAGES SOURCED &
ADDITIONAL PHOTOGRAPHY BY
Paul James

BOOK DESIGN
Robin Easter Design • Whitney Sanders

PRINTING
Jostens • Clarksville, Tennessee

PUBLISHED BY
Knoxville History Project

◆

© 2018 BY KNOXVILLE HISTORY PROJECT
516 WEST VINE AVENUE #8, KNOXVILLE, TN 37902

*All rights reserved. No part of this
publication may be reproduced in any form
without written permission from the publisher.*

PHOTO PERMISSIONS / CREDITS LISTED ON PAGE 184

ISBN 978-0-578-40636-7

EVERY EFFORT HAS BEEN MADE TO ENSURE THAT ADDRESSES, OPENING HOURS, AND CONTACT INFORMATION IS CORRECT AT THE TIME OF GOING TO PRESS. SOME DETAILS ARE LIABLE TO CHANGE INCLUDING BUSINESS LOCATIONS, OPENING TIMES, AND EXHIBITION CONTENT. PLEASE CHECK WEBSITES OR CALL AHEAD TO VERIFY INFORMATION AS NEEDED. THE KNOXVILLE HISTORY PROJECT WELCOMES COMMENTS AND SUGGESTIONS FOR FUTURE EDITIONS. PLEASE WRITE TO: KNOXVILLE HISTORY PROJECT AT 516 W. VINE AVE., KNOXVILLE TN 37902 OR EMAIL CONTACT@KNOXHISTORYPROJECT.ORG

TABLE OF CONTENTS

INTRODUCTION 1

A BRIEF HISTORY OF KNOXVILLE 3

HISTORIC HOMES ———— 20

MUSEUMS & COLLECTIONS ———— 37

DOWNTOWN ———— 45
- MAIN STREET & VICINITY ———— 45
- GAY STREET ———— 49
- THE 100 BLOCK ———— 60
- STATE STREET ———— 61
- MARKET SQUARE & VICINITY ———— 62
- THE OLD CITY ———— 64
- OFF THE GRID ———— 70

DOWNTOWN CHURCHES ———— 73

STATUES ———— 78

LITERATURE & MUSIC 82

THE CIVIL WAR ———— 89

UNIVERSITY OF TENNESSEE ———— 101

NEIGHBORHOODS ———— 115
- NORTH ———— 115
- EAST ———— 121
- SOUTH ———— 124
- WEST ———— 128

PARKS & GARDENS ———— 143
- DOWNTOWN ———— 143
- NORTH ———— 146
- EAST ———— 148
- SOUTH ———— 153
- WEST ———— 156

CEMETERIES ———— 161
- DOWNTOWN ———— 161
- NORTH ———— 166
- EAST ———— 167
- SOUTH ———— 170
- WEST ———— 171

SPONSORS 174

ABOUT KNOXVILLE HISTORY PROJECT 179

WALKING TOURS 181
ACKNOWLEDGMENTS 183
MAP KEY 186

 MAPS 188

THE KNOX COUNTY COURTHOUSE, DESIGNED BY TWO IMMIGRANTS AND COMPLETED IN 1886, HAS BEEN OPEN EVERY COURT DAY SINCE. THE FOURTH AND MOST DURABLE COURTHOUSE, IT STANDS ON THE SITE OF THE OLD PROTECTIVE FEDERAL BLOCKHOUSE OF THE 1790S.

Welcome to Historic Knoxville

Everyone sees his or her own Knoxville. Knoxville is an Appalachian city, a river city, a Southern city. Knoxville is a college town proud of its Tennessee Volunteers. It's one of the last American cities to host a World's Fair. It's the headquarters of the Tennessee Valley Authority. Knoxville is the largest city near some national institutions like the Oak Ridge National Laboratory and the Great Smoky Mountains National Park.

Peel back all these layers, though, and there's still another city here, one older and more persistent than all of its modern identities. With roots in the post-Revolutionary War era, when it became first a territorial and then a state capital, Knoxville was reborn, just before the Civil War, as a railroad-enabled center for industry and commerce and culture. It's a city that's neither Southern nor Northern, Eastern nor Western, a city of steep slopes, odd angles, and remarkable individuals who have created remarkable careers, lived remarkable lives, and left interesting marks on this perhaps most American of cities.

Whether you are a resident of Knoxville, a newcomer, or a repeat visitor, the Knoxville History Project invites you to discover the rich history of this American City. Explore its multi-faceted and dynamic downtown, learn more about your own neighborhood, and take the opportunity to visit another part of town. We hope you will be surprised, enlightened, and perhaps begin to see and understand the history and culture of Knoxville in a new light.

JACK NEELY, EXECUTIVE DIRECTOR
KNOXVILLE HISTORY PROJECT

HOLSTON TREATY STATUE ON VOLUNTEER LANDING

HERNANDO DESOTO, SEEN HERE ON HORSEBACK DISCOVERING THE MISSISSIPPI RIVER, EXPLORED THE EAST TENNESSEE REGION IN 1541

A BRIEF HISTORY OF KNOXVILLE

Before the United States, the Tennessee country was the mysterious wild place beyond the mountains, associated with Native American tribes. Prehistoric Indians of the Woodland culture settled in the immediate Knoxville area as early as 800 A.D. Much of their story is unknown. They left two mysterious mounds within what's now Knoxville's city limits.

Some centuries later, Cherokee cultures developed in the region, concentrated some 40 miles downriver along what became known as the Little Tennessee. The Cherokee probably knew the future Knoxville area mainly as a hunting ground.

Spanish explorer Hernando DeSoto ventured into the area in 1541 during his famous expedition that culminated in the European discovery of the Mississippi River. Historians surmise he came right down the north shore of the Tennessee River, directly through the future plot of Knoxville. DeSoto began 250 years of colonial-era claims by Spain, France, and England, none of whom effectively controlled the area. British explorers made their way into the region in the early 1700s, when the future Tennessee was counted as part of the Atlantic seaboard colony of North Carolina. Fort Loudoun, built in 1756 about 50 miles southwest of the future site of Knoxville, was an ill-fated attempt to establish a British fort during the French and Indian War. Hardly three years after its completion, Cherokee besieged the fort, capturing or killing most of its inhabitants.

TREATY OF HOLSTON, 1791

Spain maintained an interest in the Tennessee country for some years even after that, but never established a permanent presence. Neither did the British, though several familiar local place names, including Holston, Cumberland, and Loudoun, are remnants of the British colonial era.

Knoxville's first permanent settlers were a few families led by Revolutionary War veterans, notably James White. A former militia captain from a rural area just north of Charlotte, N.C., White (1747–1821) brought his veteran's land-grant credit to this newly opened area, nominally controlled by North Carolina.

He first settled in the area in 1785, and the following year he settled along the limestone plateau that became downtown Knoxville, and built a fort and mill along a creek first known as White's Creek, later as First Creek. His extended family, as well as several other

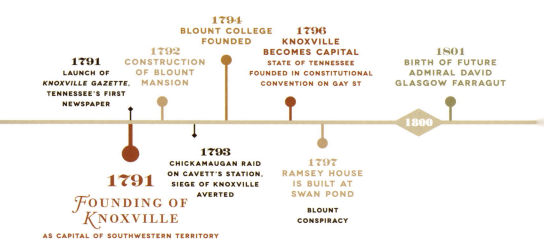

1791
LAUNCH OF *KNOXVILLE GAZETTE*, TENNESSEE'S FIRST NEWSPAPER

1792
CONSTRUCTION OF BLOUNT MANSION

1794
BLOUNT COLLEGE FOUNDED

1796
KNOXVILLE BECOMES CAPITAL
STATE OF TENNESSEE FOUNDED IN CONSTITUTIONAL CONVENTION ON GAY ST

1801
BIRTH OF FUTURE ADMIRAL DAVID GLASGOW FARRAGUT

1800

1791
FOUNDING OF KNOXVILLE
AS CAPITAL OF SOUTHWESTERN TERRITORY

1793
CHICKAMAUGAN RAID ON CAVETT'S STATION, SIEGE OF KNOXVILLE AVERTED

1797
RAMSEY HOUSE IS BUILT AT SWAN POND
BLOUNT CONSPIRACY

pioneers, created a crude settlement here. For a time, White was associated with an abortive attempt to found a new state called Franklin.

In 1791, William Blount, a Revolutionary veteran from eastern North Carolina and a signer of the U.S. Constitution, was appointed governor of the Southwestern Territory—the region not yet known as Tennessee, and formerly considered the far-west part of North Carolina.

WILLIAM BLOUNT, SIGNER OF THE U.S. CONSTITUTION

As a representative of President George Washington, he came to White's Fort in 1791 to negotiate the Treaty of the Holston with a remarkable convention of about 41 Cherokee leaders to determine the future of U.S.-Cherokee relations, at least in the near term. One of several treaties of the era, it was ultimately ineffectual, but may have allayed bloodshed for a time.

Blount soon opted to establish his permanent capital at White's Fort. It was near the Cherokee settlements, important for trading and negotiations, but not so near that the town could be destroyed without warning. The new capital's location on top of a bluff provided a defensive advantage and rendered it safe from flooding by the unpredictable river. He named it Knoxville, in honor of his immediate superior and a former general in the Revolution, Secretary of War Henry Knox.

REVOLUTIONARY WAR GENERAL HENRY KNOX

Cooperating with Blount's plans for the place, James White, with substantial help from his son-in-law Charles McClung, a surveyor from Pennsylvania, laid out a city of sorts on the flat top of the bluff. Their lottery, or allotment, of these 64 plots in October, 1791, would be remembered as the founding of Knoxville.

Blount recruited amenities like a printing press, run by George Roulstone, originally from the Boston area, who printed the territory's first law books and a newspaper called the *Knoxville Gazette*.

For the next five years, the territorial legislature met at Knoxville. Both white settlers and Native Americans—who were closer to an even match in the 1790s—had ulterior motives, and broke treaties. White soldiers under John Sevier relentlessly attacked Cherokee villages, ostensibly to defend white settlements.

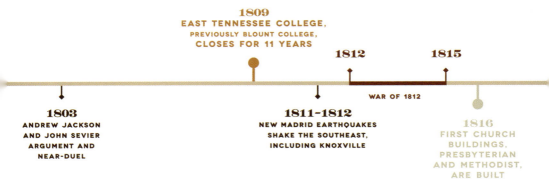

1803
ANDREW JACKSON AND JOHN SEVIER ARGUMENT AND NEAR-DUEL

1809
EAST TENNESSEE COLLEGE, PREVIOUSLY BLOUNT COLLEGE, CLOSES FOR 11 YEARS

1811–1812
NEW MADRID EARTHQUAKES SHAKE THE SOUTHEAST, INCLUDING KNOXVILLE

1812 — **1815**
WAR OF 1812

1816
FIRST CHURCH BUILDINGS, PRESBYTERIAN AND METHODIST, ARE BUILT

"UNITED STATES BARRACKS" PAINTED BY LLOYD BRANSON IN 1901, KNOXVILLE'S MAIN DEFENSIVE FORT, THE FEDERAL BLOCKHOUSE STOOD AT THE FUTURE SITE OF THE KNOX COUNTY COURTHOUSE

The radical Chickamaugan confederacy lashed back in 1793, when the white man's capital was the target of an expedition of 2,000 Chickamaugan warriors under the leadership of John Watts and the unpredictable Doublehead. They destroyed a fortified settlement on the west side of town, murdering its 13 inhabitants, including women and children. They could have done the same with Knoxville, but were discouraged by an elaborate ruse conducted by 40 white settlers, many of them non-soldiers, that led the Indians to believe the tiny city was better defended than it was. Of them, 38—to be recalled as the Invincible 38—tried to create the illusion of a large force amassed along a western ridge, while two old men remained in town, firing cannons in the blockhouse. Perceiving evidence of defenders in two directions, the Chickamaugan invaders withdrew. Knoxville was never again so threatened with obliteration.

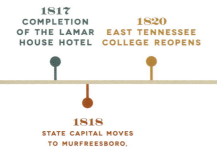

1817 COMPLETION OF THE LAMAR HOUSE HOTEL

1818 STATE CAPITAL MOVES TO MURFREESBORO, LATER NASHVILLE

1820 EAST TENNESSEE COLLEGE REOPENS

1825

1828 STEAMBOAT ATLAS ARRIVES, CONNECTING KNOXVILLE TO THE MODERN ERA OF STEAM TRAVEL

EAST TENNESSEE COLLEGE MOVES TO THE HILL

SHEEP SHEARING INCIDENT (1915) BY LLOYD BRANSON DEPICTING KNOXVILLE'S EARLIEST PRESBYTERIAN MINISTER, REV. SAMUEL CARRICK (CENTER), WITH HIS WIFE ELIZABETH CARRICK, AND TEENAGED HUGH LAWSON WHITE

Among the Invincible 38 was an unlikely warrior, taciturn, corpulent Samuel Carrick, a young Presbyterian minister from the Chesapeake Bay area—who had already started a Presbyterian church just east of town, in the Forks of the River, and developed a reputation as a doctor, perhaps just because he knew more about medicine than most of his new neighbors.

In 1794, the "strange minister," as some recalled him, started a college, an outgrowth of an informal "seminary." Carrick named it Blount College, in honor of Gov. Blount, who was among his original trustees. Later known as East Tennessee College, it was downtown, near the graveyard, and remained very small and unstable for years, but eventually evolved into a university.

In early 1796, 44 delegates from across the territory, including James Robertson of Nashville; W.C.C. Claiborne, later to be the first English-speaking governor of Louisiana; and the very young Andrew Jackson, gathered in Knoxville for three weeks to hammer out a state constitution.

Its completion on Feb. 6, 1796, believed to have taken place at the southwest corner of Gay and Church, was long observed as the birthday of Tennessee.

Although Tennesseans already considered themselves a state, statehood was formally approved by Congress the following June 1. The brash move—writing and approving a state constitution before Congress or the president had anything to say about it—is known in Puerto Rico and elsewhere as "the Tennessee plan" for statehood.

Knoxville served as Tennessee's first capital for a total of 17 years, and during that time was home to its governors, and meeting place of its legislature. One part of the U.S. Constitution was debated and approved here.

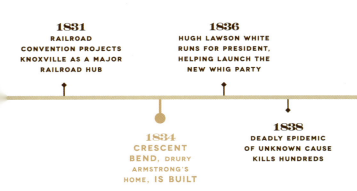

1831 RAILROAD CONVENTION PROJECTS KNOXVILLE AS A MAJOR RAILROAD HUB

1834 CRESCENT BEND, DRURY ARMSTRONG'S HOME, IS BUILT

1836 HUGH LAWSON WHITE RUNS FOR PRESIDENT, HELPING LAUNCH THE NEW WHIG PARTY

1838 DEADLY EPIDEMIC OF UNKNOWN CAUSE KILLS HUNDREDS

1844 STATE SCHOOL FOR THE DEAF ESTABLISHED, ONE OF FIRST IN AMERICA, AND CITY'S FIRST STATEWIDE INSTITUTION

AN EARLY IMAGE OF OLD COLLEGE.
EAST TENNESSEE COLLEGE'S FIRST
BUILDING ON THE HILL, BUILT IN 1828

The 12th amendment concerns the standards for electing the president and vice president. There was never a formal capitol building here—the legislature may have met in a tavern. During that period, political figures of regional and even national prominence were common sights on Gay Street, as senators, ambassadors, and a couple of presidential cabinet members lived in the tiny log-fringed hamlet of Knoxville.

East Tennessee College closed soon after the sudden death of its founder, Samuel Carrick, in 1809. It would not reopen for more than a decade. Although Carrick had founded a Presbyterian organization, he never saw his congregation build a church. Knoxville got harsh criticism in 1811 from a visiting Presbyterian cleric for its lack of a single place of worship. When Knoxville shook with the New Madrid earthquakes of 1811 and 1812, some took it as a sign.

Knoxville became a training site for the War of 1812, which drew hundreds of volunteers from the area, many of whom, like young Sam Houston, fought against the British-allied Indians at the Battle of Horseshoe Bend in the territory only later known as Alabama.

In 1816, both Presbyterian and Methodist congregations finally succeeded in building modest chapels.

By 1818, the capital logically moved toward the central part of the state, to Murfreesboro—later to move, of course, to Nashville. Without its original reason for being, Knoxvillians had to come up with something else to do. It was some years before they found it.

Meanwhile, the world of steam seemed to be passing Knoxville by. The rest of the nation was rapidly knitting itself together with steamboat and rail traffic. But steamboats had difficulty reaching Knoxville, considering the shoals and other hazards of the long,

THE DEAF AND DUMB ASYLUM, TENNESSEE'S STATE SCHOOL FOR DEAF, DURING THE CIVIL WAR, CA. 1864, WHEN IT WAS A UNION HOSPITAL

meandering Tennessee. And the mountains and rivers posed formidable obstacles to railroad construction. In comparison to the rest of the country, Knoxville became more isolated than it had been in the 1790s.

In early 1828, a light sternwheeler called the *Atlas* did make it all the way to Knoxville to collect a cash prize. It was the beginning of steamboat traffic, albeit on a limited scale, governed by the weather and the time of year. Despite some grand schemes, practical railroads remained elusive. Knoxville languished with little obvious purpose.

A partial answer arrived in 1844 in the form of a state-sponsored school for the deaf, and one of the first eight to be established in America. As a statewide institution, it was a symbolic validation for Knoxville. The Tennessee School for the Deaf became a significant presence.

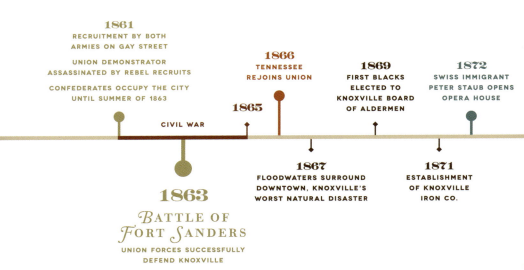

1861 RECRUITMENT BY BOTH ARMIES ON GAY STREET — UNION DEMONSTRATOR ASSASSINATED BY REBEL RECRUITS — CONFEDERATES OCCUPY THE CITY UNTIL SUMMER OF 1863

1866 TENNESSEE REJOINS UNION

1869 FIRST BLACKS ELECTED TO KNOXVILLE BOARD OF ALDERMEN

1872 SWISS IMMIGRANT PETER STAUB OPENS OPERA HOUSE

1865 CIVIL WAR

1863 BATTLE OF FORT SANDERS — UNION FORCES SUCCESSFULLY DEFEND KNOXVILLE

1867 FLOODWATERS SURROUND DOWNTOWN, KNOXVILLE'S WORST NATURAL DISASTER

1871 ESTABLISHMENT OF KNOXVILLE IRON CO.

FIRST THROUGH TRAIN FROM LOUISVILLE, KENTUCKY TO KNOXVILLE, 1883

In a real sense, modern Knoxville was born in 1855. That's when the railroad arrived, after 30 years of frustrations and failures in building railroads through the mountains and across the rivers. It brought with it hundreds of laborers, many of them Irish refugees, and inspired the city's first paved roads and streetlights, as well as a Market Square, established in 1854.

Knoxville was roaring by 1858, with freight and passenger connections to New York and other major urban markets of the East. The City had natural resources—marble, lumber, coal, iron—much in demand in the rest of the nation. Knoxville's dramatic revival was cursed with terrible timing.

No city experienced the Civil War exactly as Knoxville did, although in several ways Knox-

1879
EAST TENNESSEE UNIVERSITY BECOMES THE
UNIVERSITY OF TENNESSEE

1874
FEDERAL GOVERNMENT **BUILDS LARGE MARBLE CUSTOM HOUSE**

1885
LAWSON MCGHEE LIBRARY OPENS, TENNESSEE'S FIRST DURABLE PUBLIC LIBRARY

1875
ESTABLISHMENT OF KNOXVILLE COLLEGE FOR BLACKS, INCLUDING FORMER SLAVES

1876
TRACKS LAID FOR CITY'S FIRST STREETCARS, MULE-DRAWN

PETER KERN BUILDS BAKERY, CANDY FACTORY, AND RETAIL CENTER ON MARKET SQUARE

1882
MABRY O'CONNER GUNFIGHT LEAVES THREE DEAD, GAINS UNWELCOME NATIONAL ATTENTION

KNOX COUNTY COURTHOUSE COMPLETED

ESTABLISHMENT OF MORE LARGE FACTORIES, INCLUDING **WHITE LILY FLOUR AND BROOKSIDE MILLS**

ville's experience with the war reflected that of the whole nation. The city was home to both slaves and free blacks, and by 1850 the city's white majority had roots in both the North and the South, as well as in Western Europe.

Knoxville had slavery, but slaves were for the most part domestic servants, many of them cooks or gardeners or coachmen. Although there were some small plantations in the area, slavery was never critical to Knoxville's economy.

For some, secession fever and the war inspired loyalty to one faction or another, but also bred confusion, indecision, and fear. Some Knoxvillians tried in vain to ignore the war. Others changed sides during the course of it, sometimes more than once.

Knoxville's fiercest and most famous Unionist was newspaper editor "Parson" William G. Brownlow, a lifelong Southerner whose virulent denunciations of Secessionism got him burned in effigy as far away as Texas. His ally here was Massachusetts-born Horace Maynard, elected to Congress from Knoxville's district in 1856; a Unionist, he kept his seat in Congress even after his state seceded from the Union. Some Unionists were slaveholders, but during the war, they allied with President Abraham Lincoln and formed the core of Tennessee's Republican Party.

PARSON BROWNLOW

UNION OFFICERS ORLANDO M. POE AND ORVILLE E. BABCOCK AT FORT SANDERS, CA. 1863

Both Confederate and Union armies recruited in Knoxville, sometimes simultaneously, leading at times to street violence. Tennessee did not ally itself with the Confederacy until after the war began. An East Tennessee faction, sometimes meeting in Knoxville, threatened to secede from the state to stay in the Union.

The Confederate army had occupied Knoxville by mid-1861, even as Brownlow's *Knoxville Whig* kept publishing as the South's most pro-Union newspaper.

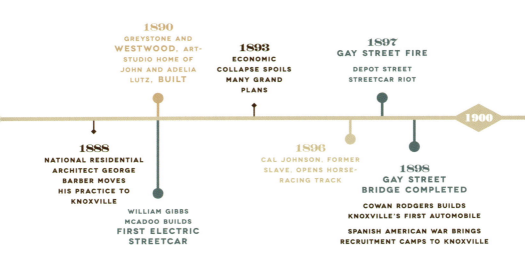

1888 NATIONAL RESIDENTIAL ARCHITECT GEORGE BARBER MOVES HIS PRACTICE TO KNOXVILLE

1890 GREYSTONE AND WESTWOOD, ART-STUDIO HOME OF JOHN AND ADELIA LUTZ, BUILT

WILLIAM GIBBS MCADOO BUILDS FIRST ELECTRIC STREETCAR

1893 ECONOMIC COLLAPSE SPOILS MANY GRAND PLANS

1896 CAL JOHNSON, FORMER SLAVE, OPENS HORSE-RACING TRACK

1897 GAY STREET FIRE
DEPOT STREET STREETCAR RIOT

1898 GAY STREET BRIDGE COMPLETED

COWAN RODGERS BUILDS KNOXVILLE'S FIRST AUTOMOBILE

SPANISH AMERICAN WAR BRINGS RECRUITMENT CAMPS TO KNOXVILLE

1900

THE SEVENTY-NINTH HIGHLANDERS FACE THE CONFEDERATE ASSAULT AT THE BATTLE OF FORT SANDERS, 1863

The Confederates occupied Knoxville for more than two years, but when those forces withdrew to assist in the battles of Chickamauga and Chattanooga, Ambrose Burnside's Union army swept in and rapidly fortified the city. What is remembered as the Battle of Knoxville was a disastrous attempt by Confederates under General James Longstreet to retake the city in November, 1863. [See Civil War]

As the war closed, occupying Unionists made a seemingly unlikely choice to be the postwar governor of Tennessee. In his first role as a public servant, at age 60, Parson Brownlow proved himself to be as effectively extreme with his political initiatives as he was with his pre-war rhetoric. Sometimes using strong-arm tactics, Gov. Brownlow forced through the passage of the 13th and 14th amendments, the parts of the U.S. Constitution forbidding slavery and assuring basic civil rights, even before these amendments were passed in most Northern states. As a consequence, Tennessee's freedmen were among America's first former slaves to be allowed to vote.

Thanks in part to Brownlow's initiatives, Tennessee did not have to deal with the

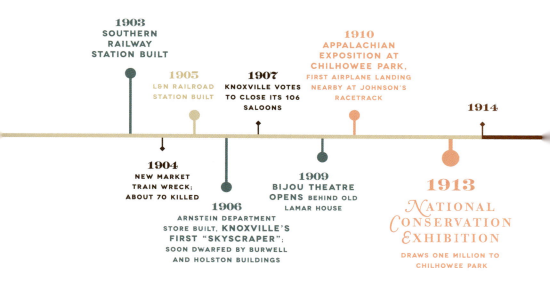

1903 SOUTHERN RAILWAY STATION BUILT

1904 NEW MARKET TRAIN WRECK; ABOUT 70 KILLED

1905 L&N RAILROAD STATION BUILT

1906 ARNSTEIN DEPARTMENT STORE BUILT, **KNOXVILLE'S FIRST "SKYSCRAPER"**; SOON DWARFED BY BURWELL AND HOLSTON BUILDINGS

1907 KNOXVILLE VOTES TO CLOSE ITS 106 SALOONS

1909 BIJOU THEATRE OPENS BEHIND OLD LAMAR HOUSE

1910 APPALACHIAN EXPOSITION AT CHILHOWEE PARK, FIRST AIRPLANE LANDING NEARBY AT JOHNSON'S RACETRACK

1913 NATIONAL CONSERVATION EXHIBITION DRAWS ONE MILLION TO CHILHOWEE PARK

1914

occupation forces associated with the Reconstruction era. Union troops left Knoxville in 1866, allowing Knoxville to return to the promise of a railroad economy that had just begun to bud before the war.

With its railroad hub, an iron mill, several marble quarries, and a couple of lumber yards, Knoxville's economy reawakened and rapidly diversified, drawing thousands more citizens. Between 1870 and 1900, Knoxville quadrupled in population, developing public schools, an opera house, a public library, electric streetcars, two train stations, two and sometimes three daily newspapers, multiple vaudeville houses, arts organizations, and baseball teams. By 1890, Knoxville was a modern American city.

With an economy based on manufacturing (iron, marble, furniture, architectural lumber,

CHILD LABORERS AT THE KNOXVILLE KNITTING MILL, CA. 1910

a wide variety of textiles, flour, beer, heavy machinery) and wholesale distributing (huge C.M. McClung & Co. offered an encyclopedic catalog with tens of thousands of products, and a reach across about a quarter of America), Knoxville was often referred to as a "metropolis," an exciting place to be, especially downtown, which had a 24-hour reputation. But it also developed the serious problems of an urban area, including a high murder rate, extreme poverty, and related problems with prostitution, addiction, and illness. Multiple progressive organizations tried to address Knoxville's issues, not always effectively. Suffragists were especially active here, and as it happened, East Tennessee played a critical role, in the evenly divided state, in passing the suffrage amendment to the U.S. Constitution.

STREETCAR ON GAY ST, 1890S

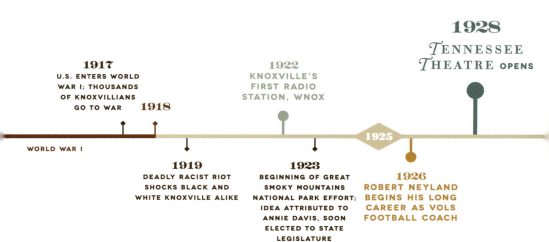

1917 U.S. ENTERS WORLD WAR I; THOUSANDS OF KNOXVILLIANS GO TO WAR

1918

WORLD WAR I

1919 DEADLY RACIST RIOT SHOCKS BLACK AND WHITE KNOXVILLE ALIKE

1922 KNOXVILLE'S FIRST RADIO STATION, WNOX

1923 BEGINNING OF GREAT SMOKY MOUNTAINS NATIONAL PARK EFFORT; IDEA ATTRIBUTED TO ANNIE DAVIS, SOON ELECTED TO STATE LEGISLATURE

1925

1926 ROBERT NEYLAND BEGINS HIS LONG CAREER AS VOLS FOOTBALL COACH

1928 TENNESSEE THEATRE OPENS

NATIONAL CONSERVATION EXPOSITION AT CHILLHOWEE PARK, 1913. ONE MILLION ATTENDED THE FIRST-OF-ITS-KIND FAIR

Knoxville's conservation movement was significant on a national scale. Artists began to express interest in the Smoky Mountains, previously little known to Knoxvillians, just as local capitalists began to realize they were running out of virgin forest to plunder, and as extremely popular President Teddy Roosevelt, a conservationist who visited Knoxville more than most presidents of his era, was extolling the virtues of preserving the forests. Conservation was a theme of three major Knoxville expositions, including the National Conservation Exposition of 1913, which drew one million visitors to Chilhowee Park.

Within a few years, a cadre of Knoxvillians, several of whom had been part of that big fair, were leading a movement, started in 1923, to create the Great Smoky Mountains National Park, a tremendously complicated undertaking involving major fundraising and thousands of separate land purchases.

Major projects were a big part of Knoxville's 20th century history. The Smokies had hardly opened before an even bigger project arrived. The unruly Tennessee River, prone to flooding, littered with treacherous shoals, and blamed for devastating agricultural erosion, became the subject of one of the most ambitious initiatives of President Franklin Roosevelt's New Deal. The government-administered Tennessee Valley Authority would commandeer riverways from Virginia to Mississippi, building dams both for flood control and hydroelectricity, creating new recreational lakes and encouraging more efficient agricultural practices.

SMOKIES PROMOTIONAL STAMP BY KNOXVILLE COMMERCIAL ARTIST, HARRY IJAMS, 1937

Knoxville became TVA's headquarters, partly because it was the city closest to their

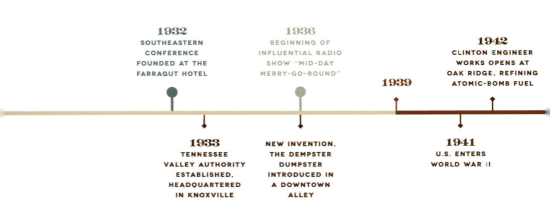

1932 SOUTHEASTERN CONFERENCE FOUNDED AT THE FARRAGUT HOTEL

1933 TENNESSEE VALLEY AUTHORITY ESTABLISHED, HEADQUARTERED IN KNOXVILLE

1936 BEGINNING OF INFLUENTIAL RADIO SHOW "MID-DAY MERRY-GO-ROUND"

NEW INVENTION, THE DEMPSTER DUMPSTER INTRODUCED IN A DOWNTOWN ALLEY

1939

1941 U.S. ENTERS WORLD WAR II

1942 CLINTON ENGINEER WORKS OPENS AT OAK RIDGE, REFINING ATOMIC-BOMB FUEL

TVA ADVERTISEMENT FROM "YOUR GUIDE TO KNOXVILLE" PROMOTIONAL BOOKLET, CA. 1940

first project, Norris Dam. TVA attracted many of America's brightest talents in conservation and forestry to Knoxville, including Benton MacKaye, already famous as founder of the Appalachian Trail, who moved to Knoxville to work for TVA. So many environmental leaders had moved to Knoxville that when the Wilderness Society, unrelated to TVA, was founded, most of its original leaders were Knoxville residents. Even the president's own youngest son, John, came to Knoxville—quietly—to work for TVA one summer. The excitement of this new experiment drew statesmen and thinkers from around the world. French philosopher Jean-Paul Sartre, Swiss architect Le Corbusier, and Indian prime minister Jawaharlal Nehru all came to Knoxville to behold TVA.

Related to TVA was another Roosevelt-administration initiative. By 1942, scientists knew of the potential of an atomic bomb. Partly to take advantage of TVA power, plentiful and already under government control, the U.S. Army started the top-secret Clinton Engineer Works, about 30 miles northwest of Knoxville. Unbeknownst to almost all citizens until August, 1945, its job was to refine radioactive uranium, elemental to the Manhattan Project.

Oak Ridge, hardly even a village before 1942, became an instant city that was, for a while, more than half as populous as Knoxville. The wartime hubbub left the ongoing legacy of the Oak Ridge National Laboratory, which brought thousands of scientists and engineers to the area. Oak Ridge's vigor stretched suburbanizing Knoxville to the west.

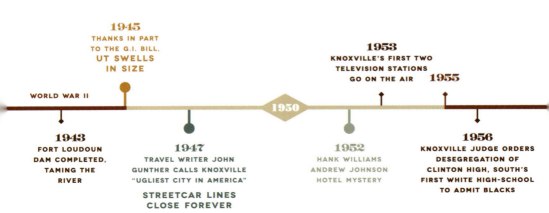

WORLD WAR II

1943 — FORT LOUDOUN DAM COMPLETED, TAMING THE RIVER

1945 — THANKS IN PART TO THE G.I. BILL, UT SWELLS IN SIZE

1947 — TRAVEL WRITER JOHN GUNTHER CALLS KNOXVILLE "UGLIEST CITY IN AMERICA" / STREETCAR LINES CLOSE FOREVER

1950

1952 — HANK WILLIAMS ANDREW JOHNSON HOTEL MYSTERY

1953 — KNOXVILLE'S FIRST TWO TELEVISION STATIONS GO ON THE AIR

1955

1956 — KNOXVILLE JUDGE ORDERS DESEGREGATION OF CLINTON HIGH, SOUTH'S FIRST WHITE HIGH-SCHOOL TO ADMIT BLACKS

Meanwhile, the University of Tennessee, fueled by the national G.I. Bill, added thousands to its rolls, and became, for the first time indisputably, a major university. And its football team under Coach Robert Neyland was a national contender, the AP National Champion in 1951.

Postwar Knoxville was a big-institution city as it had never been before. Perhaps distracted by the status, the city did little to maintain its old-fashioned core. It's an interesting historical puzzle that Knoxville seemed to wilt in the reflection of the suddenly famous attractions around it.

In 1947, respected travel author John Gunther called Knoxville "the ugliest city I have ever seen in America." In the 1950s, despite UT's growth, TVA, the popular national park, and ORNL on its

RUNDOWN OLD CITY DISTRICT ON W JACKSON AVE EARLY 1970S

doorstep, Knoxville's population declined by 10 percent, the biggest drop in its history. Suburbanization was part of the issue, as people moved out of city limits to settle in the foothills or along the suddenly flood-proof riverbanks, but several traditional industries were declining, too, especially in the marble and textile businesses.

When Knoxville lost its minor-league-baseball team in 1967, some national press suggested that Knoxville was actually suffering for its wonderful region. People weren't attending baseball games in town anymore—and perhaps not going to movies and restaurants as much either—because they were spending their free time outside of town, on the lakes or in the mountains.

Meanwhile, the city was losing some of the economic motivation for its investments in its outer regions. Towns much closer to

GEN. NEYLAND WITH HIS CHAMPION QUARTERBACK, HANK LAURICELLA, 1951

1957
JAMES AGEE'S POSTHUMOUS KNOXVILLE-BASED NOVEL, *A DEATH IN THE FAMILY*, WINS THE PULITZER PRIZE

1961
DOGWOOD ARTS FESTIVAL STARTS, COINCIDES WITH DOWNTOWN MODERNIZATIONS

CIVIC COLISEUM BUILT

1960
UT ADMITS FIRST BLACK UNDERGRADUATES

IN RESPONSE TO SIT-IN DEMONSTRATIONS, DOWNTOWN RESTAURANTS DESEGREGATE

1963
MOVIE THEATERS DESEGREGATE

VIETNAM WAR

1970
THOUSANDS OF UT STUDENTS DEMONSTRATE IN ANTIWAR STRIKES

the Smokies built large hotels and chalets and other attractions. By 1970, tourists could spend a lovely week in the Smokies without ever setting foot in Knoxville. The new interstate highways completed in the 1960s never supported the local restaurants and hotels as the old highways did. The tourist business Knoxville had just gotten used to was evaporating. What had once seemed like municipal assets were becoming distractions.

In the 1970s, the Energy Crisis gave Knoxville an excuse to contemplate a bold stroke, using the authenticity of its associations with TVA (still America's largest energy producer), UT, and ORNL, to mount a genuine world's fair, with an energy theme.

Created in a former industrial railroad yard right downtown, the 1982 World's Fair drew 23 international participants and 11 million visitors, many of whom came specifically to view one extraordinary attraction, the People's Republic of China's first-ever pavilion at a world's fair. The Fair also featured the first pavilion by a new organization not yet known as the European Union, as well as a very early public demonstration of a touch-screen computer.

The expected push that would send Knoxville into a modern future didn't arrive on schedule. The Fair had hardly been closed for three months before its chief financiers

FROM MAY 1 TO OCT. 31, 1982, KNOXVILLE'S WORLD'S FAIR ATTRACTED 11 MILLION VISITORS

were arrested and charged with bank fraud, prompting a major banking collapse and multiple prison sentences. Then, in the years just after the exposition, Knoxville witnessed the sudden growth and implosion of the niche publishing empire Whittle Communications, which closed in 1994, leaving its grand Georgian headquarters downtown, as well as hundreds of creative professionals who found reasons to stay.

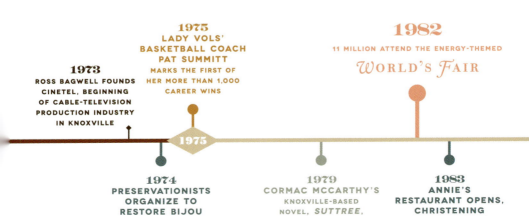

1973
ROSS BAGWELL FOUNDS CINETEL, BEGINNING OF CABLE-TELEVISION PRODUCTION INDUSTRY IN KNOXVILLE

1975
LADY VOLS' BASKETBALL COACH PAT SUMMITT MARKS THE FIRST OF HER MORE THAN 1,000 CAREER WINS

1982
11 MILLION ATTEND THE ENERGY-THEMED
World's Fair

1974
PRESERVATIONISTS ORGANIZE TO RESTORE BIJOU THEATRE; NEW ERA FOR OLD BUILDINGS

1979
CORMAC MCCARTHY'S KNOXVILLE-BASED NOVEL, *SUTTREE*, GAINS GLOBAL CULT FOLLOWING

1983
ANNIE'S RESTAURANT OPENS, CHRISTENING THE OLD CITY

Downtown limped along as it always had, albeit with a bit of new blood in the form of a couple of preservationist developers who, speculating on the fair, had reintroduced the idea of upscale urban residences. Except for a small warehouse district dubbed the Old City, downtown's revival was hard to notice until the late 1990s when larger-scale and deeper-pocketed developers were converting old commercial and industrial buildings into residential and restaurant space.

The construction of a major convention center coincided with a major renovation and expansion of the 1928 Tennessee Theatre as well as a massive infrastructure rebuild of 1854 Market Square—its flame had flickered, but never gone out.

THE "KEYHOLE" – A MARBLE INDUSTRY RELIC AT ROSS MARBLE QUARRY AT IJAMS, PART OF KNOXVILLE'S URBAN WILDERNESS

THE HOWARD H. BAKER, JR., U.S. COURTHOUSE IN THE FORMER WHITTLE BUILDING

Meanwhile, major expansions of long-obscure Ijams Nature Center into hundreds of acres of quarry land slowly being reclaimed by forest, combined with a network of bike trails throughout the city, creating the paradoxical concept of an Urban Wilderness, and suggesting a new destiny for the city as a center for outdoors adventures.

In 2009, the city welcomed an extraordinary new festival, a musical conclave so innovative and unusual that it drew international attention to the city as nothing since the World's Fair. Big Ears, aimed at the most serious music fans, regularly earns the kind of positive press that can give a city a new identity.

Something in the mix made Knoxville attractive to new sorts of businesses, first video production primarily for cable TV, (Knoxville has credibly claimed to be one of America's leading video production

1991
WHITTLE COMMUNICATIONS CONSTRUCTS GRAND NEW HEADQUARTERS BUILDING, HOME TO MULTIPLE MAGAZINES AND TELEVISION PROJECTS

1998
ARCHITECT DUANE GRIEVE RESTORES 1905 MILLER'S BUILDING

1990
KNOXVILLE MUSEUM OF ART COMPLETED

1993
REGAL CINEMAS SETTLES IN KNOXVILLE, GROWS TO BE THE WORLD'S BIGGEST CINEMA CHAIN

HGTV LAUNCHES, LED BY KEN LOWE; SCRIPPS NETWORKS BECOMES A LEADER IN KNOXVILLE'S TV INDUSTRY

MARKET SQUARE, STILL THE EPICENTER OF DOWNTOWN KNOXVILLE AFTER MORE THAN 160 YEARS

centers) and then the movie-theater business (Knoxville's Regal Cinemas was for years the largest cinema chain in the world), as well as maintaining an interesting and diverse variety of industries, including manufacturers of auto parts, medical products, chemicals, coffee, mobile homes, New York subway signs— as well as the headquarters of Pilot, which grew into a national travel-center giant during this era.

At the center of it all, assisted by the city but driven mostly by private philanthropists and developers, a compact and organically reviving downtown reoccupied long-empty old buildings. Downtown's renaissance brought movies and multiple annual festivals back to Gay Street, reintroduced Knoxville to itself, and gave the city something to do on weekends. Downtown became a popular residential neighborhood for the first time in decades. It all amounted to a reinvention of downtown for a new century. It even became, perhaps for the first time ever, a place interesting enough to draw a daily flow of tourists, who can each be overheard trying to figure the place out.

SUN RA ARKESTRA PLAY KNOXVILLE'S INTERNATIONALLY RENOWNED BIG EARS FESTIVAL

2004 MAJOR REDO OF MARKET SQUARE, MODERNIZING INFRASTRUCTURE WHILE RESTORING VICTORIAN CHARACTER

2005 IJAMS NATURE CENTER ACQUIRES HUNDREDS OF ACRES OF QUARRY LAND, DOUBLING IT IN SIZE AND MAKING IT A MAJOR OUTDOORS ATTRACTION

2011 MADELINE ROGERO ELECTED AS TENNESSEE'S FIRST FEMALE CITY MAYOR—FOLLOWING THE INTERIM ADMINISTRATION OF DANIEL BROWN, KNOXVILLE'S FIRST BLACK MAYOR

2000

2003 EAST TENNESSEE HISTORY CENTER EXPANSION COMPLETED

2005 TENNESSEE THEATRE EXPANSION AND RESTORATION COMPLETED

2009 FIRST BIG EARS FESTIVAL

HISTORIC HOMES

 ## James White's Fort

Located at 205 Hill Avenue
865-525-6514 • *jameswhitesfort.org*
MON-SAT: 9:30AM-5PM *Last tour* **AT 4PM**
WINTER: 10AM-4PM *Last tour* **AT 3PM**
Admission fee or Combo pass *

Before Knoxville existed, its bluff was the home of Revolutionary War patriot James White, who settled here with his extended family in 1786. Originally from a rural area to the north of Charlotte, White (1747–1821) was a leader among the Revolutionary land-grant settlers who arrived here during the Articles of Confederation era. He ran a mill on First Creek (in early documents the Knoxville area is sometimes known as "White's Mill") and lived with his family in a fortified stockade, in the cabin reconstructed at the southwest corner of modern-day James White's Fort.

In 1791, Governor William Blount needed to choose a spot for a territorial capital of this mostly wild territory, and picked White's Fort, of which these cabin logs are the only remnant. With Blount's encouragement, White and his son-in-law, Pennsylvania-born Charles McClung, laid out a town on the bluff. White is regarded as Knoxville's founder.

In 1796, White was a delegate to the constitutional convention that founded Tennessee. He also helped found Knoxville's first church, First Presbyterian, by making land available for it, along with the city's first graveyard. Adjacent to his original fort, the churchyard was his former turnip patch. White later served as brigadier-general of the state militia during the War of 1812. By that time, White had left his original home site in the town he founded, to live in the quieter area within walking distance to the east.

White's son, Hugh Lawson White (1773–1840) became a major figure in national politics of the 1820s and '30s, a U.S. senator who served as president pro tempore of the Senate in 1833—and, opposing his former mentor Andrew Jackson, ran for president in 1836, effectively helping to found the opposition Whig Party. He lived in this cabin as a teenager.

James White's Fort is a speculative reconstruction of that settlement, using the logs that formed James White's original cabin. One of Knoxville's most elaborate historical representations, the modern site strives to demonstrate life on the frontier in the late 19th century.

The story of how White's Fort arrived on this location is almost as interesting as its origin on the frontier. White's original fort

---

* **HISTORIC HOMES OF KNOXVILLE** *Combo pass to tour all seven house museums is available at each home*

HISTORIC HOMES

was located in a less geographically prominent spot, about one third of a mile to the northwest, on the location of the modern-day State Street garage. Almost forgotten in the 19th century, his cabin had been incorporated into urban structures for other uses before 1906, when a history-minded landowner named Isiah Ford had it disassembled into carefully numbered logs, and moved them to a suburban spot on Woodlawn Pike, across the river in South Knoxville. There it stood for about 60 years, as part of a modernized house with a wraparound porch, among other modern residences. It was an oddity mentioned, rarely, in newspaper stories.

In 1958, the city's proposal to honor White with the city's first big municipal auditorium (the Civic Coliseum was originally called the James White Memorial Auditorium) happened to coincide with the sale of the residential property on Woodlawn. Philanthropic groups purchased the cabin's old logs and reassembled them here in 1969. The fort reconstruction, employing new timber for the stockade, but historic cabins from elsewhere in the region for other structures, was completed in 1970.

Today, the fort is furnished with original artifacts and tools from the period, providing a glimpse into the daily existence of early East Tennessee settlers at the time that the city of Knoxville began. The fort's interior, planted with flowering shrubs, is probably a more beautiful place than it was in James White's time. The fort offers conducted tours of the site, including the two-story main house with its adjoining kitchen, smokehouse, guest house, and cabins occasionally featuring demonstrations by blacksmiths, spinners, and weavers.

Multiple frontier-themed public events are hosted during the year, including Statehood Day, the Fourth of July, and the Halloween-themed Hearth Scares Ball.

CA. 1800 — KNOXVILLE *was tiny but famous—it was one of only* 16 STATE CAPITALS *in America*

2 RAMSEY HOUSE

Located at 2614 Thorngrove Pike
865-546-0745 • ramseyhouse.org
WED-SAT: 10AM-4PM
Admission fee or Combo pass

Ramsey House is the second-oldest building in the Knoxville area, and is extraordinary for its stone construction, in an era of log cabins and simple frame houses.

Believed to be the first building ever constructed mostly of Tennessee marble, the house is one of only two surviving works credited to London-trained architect Thomas Hope.

Swan Pond, as it was known in the 1790s, when there was indeed a large pond nearby, was the home of Pennsylvania-raised Francis Alexander Ramsey (1764–1820), a prominent figure in early county and state government. One son, W.B.A. Ramsey, was mayor of Knoxville in the late 1830s, and was later Tennessee secretary of state. Another son, J.G.M. Ramsey, author of *Ramsey's Annals*, was arguably Tennessee's first comprehensive state historian. Both spent much of their youth in this house.

J.G.M. RAMSEY

The Ramseys left Knoxville during the Civil War—despite their Pennsylvania roots, they were secessionists—abandoning the house and eventually selling it. Upon J.G.M. Ramsey's return to town in the 1870s, he lamented the condition of the house in a poem.

First marked as a historic site by the Daughters of the American Revolution in 1927, it has been maintained as a museum house since 1952, and it is one of the most intact historic homes of its era, including several original furnishings including furniture made by Tennessee's earliest cabinetmakers. The collection also includes Chippendale antiques once owned by the Ramseys. Vintage "Base Ball" games in period uniforms are staged on the grounds during warmer months. Playing by 1864 rules and adopting original Knoxville team names adds authenticity to this distinctly American historical re-enactment.

Overall, the site now encompasses more than 100 acres including a Visitor Center and picnic areas.

The FIRST BUILDING OF TENNESSEE MARBLE, *Ramsey House (1797) stands near old quarries*

Blount Mansion

Located at 200 West Hill Avenue
865-525-2375 • *blountmansion.org*
**SPRING-FALL TUES-FRI: 9:30AM-5PM
SAT: 10AM-2PM • WINTER HOURS VARY**
Admission fee or Combo pass

Built in 1792, Blount Mansion has been claimed to be the first frame house built west of the Appalachian Mountains. Its survival is remarkable, considering that in 1925 it was a slum, almost razed for parking for the nearby Andrew Johnson Hotel project.

It was the home of territorial Governor William Blount and his wife, Mary, who is believed to have had some influence on its Eastern-style design, with glass windows then rare in this part of the country. According to tradition, the Native Americans called it "the House with Many Eyes."

William Blount lived here for most of his gubernatorial tenure, and presumably entertained exotic guests here, like influential botanist Andre Michaux and—though proof is sketchy—future "Citizen King" Louis Philippe, who was at least briefly in Knoxville in 1797. The Blounts also lived here at the time of the Tennessee's first constitutional convention in 1796, in which Blount played a leading role, and during his short tenure as one of the new state's first U.S. senators—abbreviated by accusations of treason, prompted by the discovery of Blount's involvement in a complicated plot to enlist British help to seize Spanish Louisiana. He died here in 1800, his wife two years later.

The house was later home to the confusingly named Willie (pronounced "Wiley") Blount, William Blount's much-younger half-brother, who lived here when he served as third governor of Tennessee, 1809 to 1815. Willie Blount expanded the house significantly.

Still later, the landmark was home to the

Of Knoxville's approximately 200 houses in 1800, Blount Mansion is the only survivor

Boyd family, which included Samuel Beckett Boyd, mayor of Knoxville from 1847 to 1851. Reputed Confederate spy Belle Boyd stayed here in the dramatic summer of 1863. The Boyds remodeled the house with Victorian flourishes, including a broad porch.

The house, neglected or forgotten as a landmark, became a flophouse in the early 20th century, and word that it was going to be demolished was mourned by only a few.

However, a renovation effort led by neighbor Mary Boyce Temple brought it to the public's attention, and by the end of the 1920s, it was a much-visited shrine.

The word "Mansion" may seem misleading. It's actually a small house, simple in construction, suggesting a life of bare essentials. The word was probably applied in retrospect to indicate that it was the home of governors. The house has been subject to multiple interpretations and architectural research over the years. Current scholarship suggests that William and Mary Blount lived very simply here, albeit with the help of slaves.

The house was actually made of sawn lumber to meet Mary Blount's requirement of "a proper wooden house." The detached kitchen is a recreation of a common

eighteenth-century kitchen, located on the site of the original structure. The Governor's Office was a typical "law office" of the 1790s, built right on the edge of State Street. The cooling shed was excavated during an archaeological dig in the 1950s, and the shed roof was rebuilt under the supervision of the National Park Service. Blount Mansion is today Knoxville's only National Landmark, a building federally protected from destruction.

Throughout the year, Blount Mansion offers a wide variety of programs highlighting significant revolutionary-related themes, as well as legends, customs, and myths, particularly around Halloween and the Christmas season.

One of BLOUNT'S VISITORS *here was French botanist-spy* ANDRÉ MICHAUX

Marble Springs

Located at 1220 West Governor John Sevier Highway • 865-573-5508
marblesprings.net
WED–SAT: 10AM–5PM • SUN: NOON–5PM
Admission fee or Combo pass

A humble complex of log cabins in a clearing in the South Knox County woods, Marble Springs is off John Sevier Highway, and very near Neubert Springs, a popular rural resort in the late 19th and early 20th century. It's no "governor's mansion", but it was the longtime home of the state's first governor, John Sevier (1745–1815). Revolutionary War hero of the critical Battle of King's Mountain in 1780, Sevier was an Indian fighter and sometime congressman known for his role in the abortive State of Franklin and the early days of Tennessee. Born in Northern Virginia of recent French ancestry, Sevier and his also heroic wife, Bonnie Kate (1754–1836)—her boldness in the face of Indian attacks made her the subject of early folklore, herself—lived on this patch of land by 1796, when he became the state's first governor. Although Sevier began construction on a proper town home—now known as the James Park House—he never completed it. Apparently, he had no complaints about living out here, an hour's ride from the capital at Knoxville.

Sevier was prominent in early Tennessee history, and even in American folklore—his rift with Andrew Jackson is believed to have had generations-long repercussions in the state's political divide, and Teddy Roosevelt was fascinated with his example as a bold and ruthless frontiersman. However, his physical legacy is almost ghostly. He died on a surveying expedition in the Alabama wilderness, and his grave was missing for 70 years, before some scant remains were reburied at the courthouse *(see p.46)*. The site of his rural home, Marble Springs, became a historic site in 1941, the year of Knoxville's sesquicentennial, when a log cabin that had long been credibly identified as Sevier's was restored.

GOVERNOR JOHN SEVIER

Not always rustic, Congressman **JOHN SEVIER** *was a* **FREQUENT GUEST** *at the* **MADISON WHITE HOUSE**

HISTORIC HOMES

However, in 2007, University of Tennessee researchers employed dendrochronological analysis to determine the cabin's age, and concluded that none of its logs were older than 1835, 20 years after Sevier's death. Still, that makes it one of the oldest original-site log cabins in the area, and considering most of his world has vanished, no other site is so intimately associated with Sevier.

The cabins are arranged on the site to suggest how the Seviers' farm might have appeared over 200 years ago. Even if there are no actual logs John and Bonny Kate Sevier ever touched, they would have recognized this hillside, and the general appearance of the place. Two other cabins from rural spots in Knox County complete the complex. The Walker Cabin, moved here from Walker Springs Road in suburban West Knoxville, dates to 1828.

JOHN SEVIER'S TRUNK

Unlike other historic homes, Marble Springs is a rustic, mostly outdoor experience. Depending on the time of year, it's a place for stargazing, easter-egg hunts, and "ice-cream socials."

Restless JOHN SEVIER *died at age* 70 *on an* EXPEDITION *into the* ALABAMA WILDERNESS

Crescent Bend

*Located at 2728 Kingston Pike
865-637-3163 • crescentbend.com*
WED-FRI: 10AM-4PM ♦ SAT: 10AM-2PM
Admission fee or Combo pass

Cresent Bend, also known as the Armstrong-Lockett House, stands out more from the river, which it meets with its gracefully terraced lawns, than from the street. Built in 1834, it was the home of Drury Paine Armstrong (1799–1856), who once owned almost 1,000 acres on both sides of the river. His son, Robert Houston Armstrong, a lover of art and literature who grew up in this house, built Bleak House, just west of here, and later helped build Westwood.

Seized by the rebel army in 1863, Crescent Bend was briefly the headquarters of Confederate Gen. Joseph Kershaw, who commanded troops during the siege of Fort Sanders.

The Armstrong family kept the house until the 1890s, when a new owner bought it and attempted to convert it into a stylish Victorian-style home, with more porches and a turret. After that fashion had passed, later owners restored Armstrong's original design. The Toms Foundation, founded by philanthropist William Perry "Buck" Toms (for whom the region's Boy Scout camp is also named) purchased the property, and on the nation's bicentennial, July 4, 1976, opened Crescent Bend to the public as a museum house. It's especially noted for its silver collection, dating back to the 1500s, as well as some notable historical portraits.

Crescent Bend's **ANTEBELLUM FRENCH WALLPAPER** *was salvaged from a* **BURNING RIVERBOAT**

HISTORIC HOMES

Bleak House

Located at 3148 Kingston Pike 865-522-2371 • bleakhouseknoxville.org • MAR-DEC WED: 1-3:30PM OR BY APPOINTMENT *Admission fee • Privately owned, not a member of the Historic Homes of Knoxville*

Also known as "Confederate Memorial Hall," this Tuscany-style villa is owned and managed by the United Daughters of the Confederacy. Its builder, Robert Houston Armstrong, named it after Charles Dickens' 1853 novel.

The home served as the headquarters for Gen. James Longstreet and Gen. Lafayette McLaws, during the Siege of Knoxville from November 17 – December 4, 1863. Particularly noteworthy is the eerie tower featuring cannonball holes, and a sketch of three Confederate sharpshooters who were killed or wounded here. The legend that Gen. Sanders was killed by a shot from this tower is explored in David Madden's 1996 novel, *Sharpshooter*.

It was a private residence until purchased by the United Daughters of the Confederacy in 1959, in time for centennial celebrations. They renamed the place Confederate Memorial Hall. Part of UDC's mission is to commemorate the Confederacy. Although the battle-scarred house and its terraced gardens are used for meetings and especially known for weddings, tours are available by appointment.

A notable collection of paintings by Knoxville artist Eleanor McAdoo Wiley, sister of Catherine Wiley, are featured throughout the house.

When his KNOXVILLE SIEGE *failed so miserably,* GEN. LONGSTREET OFFERED *to* RESIGN

Mabry-Hazen House

*Located at 1711 Dandridge Avenue
865-522-8661 • mabryhazen.com*
MON-FRI: 11AM-5PM • SAT: 10AM-3PM
Admission fee or Combo pass

The Mabry-Hazen House is a historic home with an unusually personal story, one of three generations of a dramatic and sometimes violent family. Joseph Mabry II was a business speculator who in 1853 made a formal real-estate proposal (along with co-owner William Swan and the city) that quickly became what we know today as Market Square. It was not long afterward, in 1858, that he constructed this handsome if melancholy wooden home with wraparound porches and a hilltop view of the city of Knoxville. A slave owner, Mabry had been a generous supporter of the Confederacy early in the war, and hosted Confederate Gen. Felix Zollicoffer here in 1861. But as a pragmatic businessman, Mabry offered his services to the Union army upon its arrival in September, 1863, and Mabry Hill became a fortified part of the Union defense. For the Mabrys, the postwar period was more dramatic, and more dangerous.

JOSEPH MABRY II

At Christmastime in 1881, Mabry's son Will was shot to death in a saloon fight on Gay Street by a man named Lusby. In a courthouse fracas, Mabry and another son, Joseph, allegedly killed Lusby and his father. Only weeks later, Mabry made a threat to banker Thomas O'Conner, whom Mabry resented for possible complicity in Will's death. On Oct. 19, 1882, the two confronted each other on Gay Street in front of O'Conner's Mechanics Bank. O'Conner shot and killed Mabry, as Mabry's son, Joseph III, approached and shot O'Conner—as O'Conner shot young Mabry. All three men died almost simultaneously, as the result of a feud that had left six men shot to death over a period of 10 months. The fatal triple shooting earned national press. *(see p.56).*

Mabry's widow and other descendants lived on in the house for almost a century after the gunfight. The last resident was Mabry's granddaughter, "Miss Evelyn" Hazen, a never-married schoolteacher and literary secretary who in 1934 became famous—or, to some bounders, infamous—when she sued a prosperous young Knoxville man with whom she'd had sexual relations for breaking his promise to marry her. The rare "breach of promise" case once again brought the Mabrys unwelcome national press. She won the case, but never collected the settlement.

Most of the Mabry-Hazen home has changed little since its construction, and presents an authentic setting to consider the tale of a willful family. The marble mantels are especially notable. Bethel Cemetery, downhill to the north, also known as the Confederate Cemetery, is administered by the Mabry-Hazen House and can be part of the experience *(see p.167).*

THREE RESIDENTS *of the Mabry-Hazen house died in* **GAY STREET GUNFIGHTS** *in less than a year*

HISTORIC HOMES

 WESTWOOD

Located at 3425 Kingston Pike
865-523-8008 • historicwestwood.org
MON-THURS: 10AM-4PM

Designed by Baumann Brothers and built of brick and stone, Westwood stood apart from other Victorian homes even when it was built in 1890, during the extravagant height of architecture's Richardsonian Romanesque period. It drew attention because it was designed specifically for a working artist. Adelia Armstrong Lutz (1859–1931) had grown up across the street at Bleak House. After she studied painting technique at the Corcoran in Washington and the Pennsylvania Academy in Philadelphia, then independently in impressionism-era Paris, her work had gotten attention at several expositions. Hoping marriage and motherhood wouldn't interfere with her potential, her father Robert Houston Armstrong, a talented artist himself, and her insurance-executive husband, John Lutz, got together to build her this remarkable house, with a large personal studio with high ceilings and skylights, offering an unlimited supply of natural light. Here she worked as an artist for 40 years, painting portraits and still lifes while raising two children and occasionally hosting meetings of the vigorous Nicholson Art League, which ambitiously promoted art in galleries and local expositions.

ADELIA ARMSTRONG LUTZ

She was especially fond of hollyhocks, which appeared in her paintings and in her yard.

Considered a country house in a day when it stood alone outside of city limits and beyond the connections of streetcars and sidewalks, the extraordinary home drew press attention in its time for its unique studio room. Today Westwood may be Knoxville's best-preserved example of the high Victorian style of architecture—restored, yes, to some degree, but partly just kept as it was. The studio's fireplace includes tile portraits, most of them faded, of Adelia's favorite authors.

The wooden grand staircase is impressive, lit from the outside by stained-glass windows, but servants used another, narrower one, behind it. The simple kitchen is named for the Lutz's longtime maid, Sally. The serpentine wall out front was a later addition, from 1930, when the noise and fumes of cross-country automobile traffic along what was then becoming known as the Dixie-Lee Highway were just beginning to be a bother.

The house remained in Adelia's family into the 21st century; among its residents were a progressive physician and bookstore owners, all of whom honored the home's heritage by changing it little. Purchased by the Aslan Foundation, Westwood has served since 2013 as the headquarters of vigorous preservationist nonprofit Knox Heritage, which uses Adelia's capacious studio for public programs and memorable fundraisers. Tours of the home are free, but donations are encouraged.

ADELIA LUTZ *painted portraits and still lifes in this* NATURALLY LIT STUDIO *for* 40 *years*

THE LARGE READING ROOM WAS THE FEDERAL COURT ROOM FROM 1874 TO 1934

MUSEUMS & COLLECTIONS

 ### East Tennessee History Center

Located at 601 South Gay Street
865-215-8830 • easttnhistory.org
MON–FRI: 9AM–4PM • SAT: 10AM–4PM
SUN: 1–5PM *Free on Sundays and children under 16*

RECONSTRUCTION OF ALBERS CORNER DRUGSTORE

The East Tennessee Historical Society was founded in 1834, but it wasn't until the 1990s that the 35-county organization developed its first museum, in the marble 1874 Custom House building that had once housed the city's main post office and federal courts. In 2003, the building underwent a major expansion, reaching to Gay Street, its new entrance, growing exhibit and storage space and making room for a gift shop and auditorium along the way. Owned by the Knox County Public Library, the facilities are partly managed by ETHS, which runs the densely displayed "Voices of the Land" chronological exhibit of several centuries of East Tennessee, from Chattanooga to Bristol. Included is a recreation of a downtown drugstore from the late 1800s, a restored Island Home streetcar, Davy Crockett's rifle, moments in sound and video from Knoxville's country-music heyday, memories of the early days of the Great Smoky Mountains

ISLAND HOME STREET CAR

National Park and the 1982 World's Fair, and a real rarity, the desk used by Rep. Horace Maynard when he was in U.S. Congress representing a congressional district located in a state that had seceded.

On the second floor is the Knox County Archives, and on the third floor, the McClung Collection, a trove of old books, articles, and stories about the entire region. The old courtroom where Wild West outlaw Harvey "Kid Curry" Logan faced federal charges for months—before escaping from jail in 1903, never to be seen again—is now the elegant, quiet Reading Room.

Its digital collections, including the famous Thompson Photographic Collections, are at *cmdc.knoxlib.org.*

The History Center also houses the subterranean chambers of the Tennessee Archive of Moving Image and Sound, part of Knox County Public Library, whose ongoing mission is to collect and make available early film and audio recordings relevant to area history since the beginning of recording technology. For more information contact *tamis@knoxlib.org.*

Unusual in its scope, the **MCCLUNG COLLECTION** *draws researchers from* **MULTIPLE STATES**

② BECK CULTURAL EXCHANGE CENTER

Located at 1927 Dandridge Avenue
865-524-8461 • *beckcenter.net*
TUES–SAT: 10AM–6PM

The Beck Center is part museum, part archive, part gathering place, all with a focus on the African-American experience in Knoxville. Its comfortable location, a 1912 house on Dandridge Avenue, is especially apt, a celebration of history that's historic in itself. It was the final home of black Knoxville's power couple of the 20th century. James Beck, a teacher and also Tennessee's first postal clerk, co-founded the National Association for the Advancement of Colored People, then the nation's leading civil-rights activist organization, in 1919. His wife Ethel, a nationally recognized tennis champ, was a philanthropist who supported the local black orphanage. Throughout their 56-year marriage, they were a successful and stylish couple who inspired the black community, even in an era of strict segregation, to aim high. Their bequest made the Beck Center possible.

A gallery of photographs tells the story of Knoxville's civil-rights era. A gift shop includes books about the black experience. Artifacts on display date back to the era of slavery. One upstairs room serves as an instructive shrine to Judge William Hastie, the former Knoxvillian who became a pioneer black federal judge—and the first black governor, of the U.S. Virgin Islands, in the 1940s. The Beck hosts regular events, including lectures, parties, and movie screenings.

The **BECK CENTER** *is less than half a mile down the street from* **HALEY HERITAGE SQUARE**

Knoxville Museum of Art

Located at 1050 Worlds Fair Park Dr
865-525-6101 • knoxart.org
TUES–SAT: 10AM–5PM • SUN: 1–5PM

The Knoxville Museum of Art, built in 1990 on the approximate site of the Japan Pavilion during the World's Fair, was one of the last works designed by notable museum architect Edward Larrabee Barnes. Faced with local Tennessee marble, the museum always hosts changing exhibits, but its signature exhibition, "Higher Ground: A Century of Visual Arts in East Tennessee" demonstrates about 170 years of artistic history in a chronological format, ranging from early landscapes to Knoxville impressionist Catherine Wiley to African-American abstract-expressionist Beauford Delaney—and his very different brother, Joseph—as well as later works by notable abstract artists associated with the university. Other artists highlighted include Lloyd Branson (Knoxville's first professional artist, whose era spanned from the post Civil War period to the 1920s); still-life and portrait painter Adelia Lutz; Charles Krutch ("the Corot of the South"); colorful realist Charles Griffin Farr; and modernists Robert Birdwell, Carl Sublett, and C. Kermit "Buck" Ewing.

**LANDSCAPE REDESIGNED (1943)
BY C. KERMIT "BUCK" EWING**

YADDO (1950) BY BEAUFORD DELANEY

**BELLE ISLE FROM LYONS VIEW
(1859) BY JAMES CAMERON**

The Knoxville Museum of Art offers **LECTURES AND FILMS** *but also* **NIGHTCLUB-STYLE MUSICAL EVENTS**

McClung Museum of Natural History and Culture

*Located at 1327 Circle Park Drive
865-974-2144 • mcclungmuseum.utk.edu* • **MON–SAT: 9AM–5PM • SUN: 1–5PM**

A Smithsonian Affiliate museum, the McClung offers a fascinating array of permanent and temporary exhibits featuring history and the arts. Founded to preserve Native American finds disturbed by TVA's dam building projects, McClung still makes that a specialty. But it also includes permanent exhibits ranging from paleontology to Ancient Egypt to Knoxville's experience with the Civil War, with rotating exhibits on a wide array of subjects, especially artworks from across the centuries and around the world.

"The Civil War in Knoxville: The Battle of Fort Sanders exhibit" covers the bloodiest battle in the Knoxville Campaign on November 29, 1863. Key artifacts include a drum found in Gen. Longstreet's camp, a cane once belonging to Abraham Lincoln, and namesake Frank H. McClung's pardon signed by fellow Tennessean President Andrew Johnson.

Also worth a look for a broader historical perspective is the museum's flagship exhibit, *Archaeology and the Native Peoples of Tennessee*, tracing the past 12,000–15,000 years of Native American occupation of Tennessee, featuring prehistoric Native American art.

Ever-surprising **MCCLUNG MUSEUM** *includes some local dinosaur remains, like those of the* **EDMONTOSAURUS**

MUSEUMS & COLLECTIONS

 ## John C. Hodges Library

*Located at 1015 Volunteer Boulevard
865-974-4351 • lib.utk.edu •* **SPECIAL COLLECTIONS MON–FRI: 9AM–5:30PM**

The John C. Hodges Library's modernist cascade of brick cubes is a striking part of any walk around campus. But that spectacle conceals a fascinating and functional resource, not just for students and faculty but for anyone who's ever curious about nearly anything. Within this capacious building are more than 3 million items, ranging from Renaissance-era Italian printings more than 500 years old to this week's *UT Daily Beacon*. Among its collections are the personal papers of a variety of major figures, including Pulitzer-winning writer James Agee, Hollywood director Clarence Brown (a 1910 alum), and author Alex Haley, who often lectured at UT in his later years and was familiar with this building. Also here is a wide variety of memorabilia from one of the region's oldest and largest universities, including yearbooks dating back to the 19th century and a huge collection of photographs concerning the early development of the Great Smoky Mountains National Park. Some of these intrepid photographers, like Jim Thompson, helped develop the park, vividly recording the flora and fauna of the mountains, and a landscape still unfamiliar to most. And always there is UT's academic Hall of Fame, an original bust of Haley, and a head-scratching crypto-archaeological exhibit, the Centaur of Volos.

Lectures in the library's public auditorium feature statesmen, scholars, national poets laureate, and occasional rock stars. Ever-changing public exhibits range in subject from impressionism to popular music to global war.

Many of the library's resources don't even require a visit. The library's extensive online resources include much of its photographic collection as well as its ancient yearbooks and fading football programs.

Among the library's rarities is **PRESIDENT ANDREW JACKSON'S FAMILY BIBLE**

6. Farragut Museum

Located at 11408 Municipal Center Drive • 865-966-7057 townoffarragut.org/186/farragut-museum • MON–FRI: 10AM–4:30PM

The Farragut Memorial Plaza features a bronze statue and now a historical marker from his birthplace near Admiral Farragut Park off Northshore Drive.

This small community museum covers the life of Farragut, with some of his personal possessions including Farragut's shipboard desk from the *USS Hartford* and artifacts of his era, including a rare Civil War naval-battle scrimshaw set; a description and relics of the local Civil War skirmish, the Battle of Campbell's Station, at the beginning of the Confederate siege of Knoxville in 1863; and nostalgic reminders of the days of cross-country tourism, when, between about 1917 and 1965, Kingston Pike was part of two national pre-Interstate highway routes, the junction of the Dixie and Lee Highways. Also included are historic displays related to the community of Concord.

7. Women's Basketball Hall of Fame

Located at 700 Hall of Fame Drive 865-966-7057 • *wbhof.com* MON–SAT: 10AM–5PM

The Women's Basketball Hall of Fame, at the southern end of Hall of Fame drive was built with an extraordinarily unusual design, including what some claim to be the world's largest basketball as its roof. The museum appeared on downtown's southeastern corner in 1999. Inspired by the example of UT coach Pat Head Summitt and her Lady Vols (Summitt was one of the first inductees), it

FARRAGUT *is a Hispanic name; the* ADMIRAL'S FATHER *was a* SEAMAN *from* MINORCA

includes a dynamic 17-foot statue of basketball players in mid-jump, the basis for the award given to winners of the distinction. The

hall currently includes about 150 women, and a few men, who have distinguished themselves in the sport since its earliest days, with a narrative display laying out the history of the sport, with exhibits of equipment and uniforms, as well as an actual basketball court that invites visitors to take a shot. The sport has a deep history in Knoxville, where women played basketball before they could vote.

 ## Girl Scout Museum at Daisy's Place

Located at 1567 Downtown West Blvd
865-689-9835 • *girlscoutcsa.org*
MON-FRI: 9AM-5PM

Located at the Girl Scouts of the Southern Appalachians in West Knoxville, Daisy's Place Museum features vintage Girl Scout uniforms, memorabilia, and interpretive displays. The archival library includes publications, newsletters, and historical papers dating back to 1912.

 ## Knox County Museum of Education

Located at 801 Tipton Avenue
865-579-8264 • *kcme.website*
MON-FRI: 11AM-5PM

Located at the Sarah Simpson Professional Development Technology Center, the museum showcases the history of Knox County and Knoxville City Schools. Featured are yearbooks, histories, records, memorabilia, and historical photographs. Records date back to 1820.

 ## Arnstein Jewish Community Center

Located at 6800 Deane Hill Drive
865-690-6343 • *jewishknoxville.org*
MON-FRI: 9AM-5PM • SUN: 10AM-5PM

MAX AND LALLA ARNSTEIN

On the west side of Bearden, the Arnstein Jewish Community Center has been here in this modern building since 1968, replacing a previous downtown building. Its original 1929 founders were dynamic merchant-philanthropist Max Arnstein, who built Knoxville's first "skyscraper" in 1906, and his wife, Lalla, who in 1924 became the first female elected to county government. The Arnstein contains archives of the local Jewish community and the Schwarzbart Gallery, named after architect and artist Arnold Schwarzbart, which hosts art exhibits.

Successful merchant **MAX ARNSTEIN** *died in 1961, at age 102*

LOOKING SOUTH ON GAY ST, RECOGNIZED BY THE AMERICAN PLANNING ASSOCIATION AS ONE OF THE "GREAT PLACES IN AMERICA"

DOWNTOWN

Downtown Knoxville looks different from most reviving downtowns. Part of it's the scale. These streets are narrow. Especially on Gay Street, the ratio of building height to street width is striking. Even Market Square isn't square at all, but an oblong rectangle.

Part of it's the topography. Most of downtown Knoxville is on top of a steep bluff. Some downtown streets require downshifting. Several buildings have useful space, with windows, three floors below the street level.

And it's all very concentrated. Everything—the historic theaters; the county; state, and federal courthouses; city and county government; all the banks; the cinema complex; 50-odd restaurants and bars; five churches; two public libraries; a museum; about eight hotels; and perhaps 3,000 residences—are in the same half-square mile patch.

Its peculiarities reflect its history. Downtown Knoxville is on exactly the same street grid laid out in 1791. When most buildings were only two stories tall, and most commuters were pedestrians, these streets seemed sufficiently broad. And only in the early 1790s did it seem prudent to put a capital city on top of a steep hill, for defense against Indian factions who sought to destroy the white man's capital.

As it happened, defense was a less urgent issue by 1800 after the Indian threat had lifted—but the city was already up here, and here it stayed. Of course, altitude also eliminated the risk of flooding, an annual reality across much of the Tennessee Valley until a network of TVA dams was completed, over 75 years ago.

That hilltop spot between Clinch Avenue and the river that was once the capital of Tennessee is the oldest part of Knoxville. Very little remains from the capital era, 1791 to 1818. Overlooking the river is Blount Mansion (*see p.24*), just off Gay Street on West Hill Avenue. Reputedly the first frame house ever built west of the Appalachians, it's the rare survivor of the era when Knoxville was an administrative center. Just east of there is the reconstruction of James White's Fort (*see p.20*).

MAIN STREET & VICINITY

 ### OLD COURTHOUSE

Located at 300 Main Street
865-215-2385 • *knoxcounty.org*
MON-FRI: 8AM-4:30PM

This courthouse is the most durable of four courthouses around the intersection of Gay and Main since the 1790s. It's a late-Victorian creation, dating to 1884–86, designed by Stephenson & Getaz, local architects from England and France respectively—based on a Palliser & Palliser pattern. In days before air-conditioning, crowds often formed on the lawn to witness high-profile cases through the open windows. The courthouse's tower holds the "Cheshire clock" visible from the river and referenced in Cormac McCarthy's novel *Suttree*.

Gay Street once **HOSTED NINE** *separate* **MOVIE THEATERS**

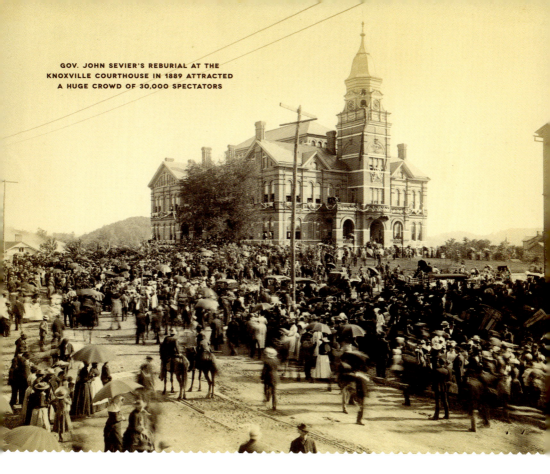

GOV. JOHN SEVIER'S REBURIAL AT THE KNOXVILLE COURTHOUSE IN 1889 ATTRACTED A HUGE CROWD OF 30,000 SPECTATORS

The soldier statue commemorates the Spanish-American War, as do the "cannons", which make a peculiar story. Originally they were captured Spanish cannons from that war, perhaps donated to the city at the time of Admiral Dewey's visit in 1900. The county chose to contribute them to a World War II scrap drive. They were missed, though, and some 50 years later, county government chose to replace them with fiberglass replicas.

The marble porte-cochère at Cumberland and Main is a memorial to "Our Beloved Physician," Dr. John Mason Boyd (1833–1909), known for his expertise in obstetrics.

The lawn of the courthouse is a burial place, albeit with unusual circumstances. It holds the grave of Revolutionary War hero, Indian fighter, and first governor of Tennessee, John Sevier. But what was buried here in 1889, before 30,000 spectators, were only a few bones. Sevier was a 70-year-old congressman on a surveying expedition on land acquired after the War of 1812 when he died and was

THE OLD COURTHOUSE LAWN AT GAY ST AND MAIN ST WITH JOHN MASON BOYD MEMORIAL PORTE-COCHÈRE

Frontier hero **JOHN SEVIER** *was a bitter enemy of* **ANDREW JACKSON**

GOV. JOHN SEVIER MEMORIAL

buried in the wilderness of what was only later known as Alabama.

Sevier's grave was missing for years, but in the 1880s a new appreciation of Sevier's legacy coincided with the construction of a new courthouse, and a movement led by Gov. Robert Taylor resulted in the exhumation of what little remained of Sevier, and a reburial here in 1889. Some 33 years later, his famous wife Bonnie Kate was disinterred from her original grave elsewhere in Alabama, and reburied alongside Sevier.

The courthouse is still used for several public purposes, but today most trials are held in the adjacent City County Building, a large modernist concrete building designed in 1978 by McCarty Holsaple McCarty.

 ## Post Office

Located at 505 Main Street
MON–FRI: 7:30AM–5PM

To the west along Main Street and across the street is the old U.S. Post Office and federal courthouse building. Designed by Baumann and Baumann in 1932, it's believed to show the influence of French-born architect Paul Cret. One of downtown's best buildings to show off the area's distinctive pink marble, it becomes pinker when wet! The marble eagles across the pediment are perhaps the best-known architectural work of Italian-immigrant stone carver Albert Milani, who worked in Knoxville for 60 years, much of it at Candoro Marble in South Knoxville.

1934 U.S. POST OFFICE BUILDING, NOW TENNESSEE SUPREME COURT BUILDING

Among the judges' decisions handed down in this building, perhaps none were more significant than Judge Robert Taylor's 1956 ruling that Clinton High School, 25 miles northwest of Knoxville, would have to desegregate immediately, making it the first school in the South to do so. The decision got immediate national attention—and unfortunately drew segregationist militants from across the country, and elicited some dynamite bombings.

MARBLE SCULPTOR ALBERT MILANI

Several **ITALIAN STONECUTTERS** *moved to Knoxville to work with* **LOCAL MARBLE**

Some militants, like former New Yorker John Kasper, were tried for federal crimes, in this same court house, facing the same judge whose decision had set it all in motion. It's no longer the federal court, but the strikingly decorative second-floor courtroom is now used by the Tennessee Supreme Court.

③ On the corner of Main and Locust Avenue, the **MEDICAL ARTS BUILDING**, a 1931 Gothic Revival-style building intended for physicians and dentists, now offers a mixture of residential and business use.

Just off Main Street are some other notable buildings. Walnut Street used to be called Crooked Street, and the reason it was crooked was that it had to go around the **JAMES PARK HOUSE**, at Cumberland and Walnut. It was conceived as a home for John Sevier, back in the days when even a nationally prominent governor and congressman sometimes went broke. When Sevier had to give up on the structure, it was completed in 1812 by Irish immigrant James Park. A literary fellow who sometimes wrote book reviews, Park became Knoxville's second (and fourth!) mayor. His son, Presbyterian minister James Park, was born in this house and died here, 90 years later. In the 20th century, it served several health-related purposes, including as the first local

YWCA, CLINCH AVE AT WALNUT ST

YMCA, CLINCH AVE AND LOCUST ST

headquarters of the Red Cross. During World War I, hundreds of women worked here making bandages and cold-weather garments for soldiers in Europe. In recent years, the handsomely renovated home (not open to the public) has served as the headquarters of Gulf & Ohio, a short-line railroad.

⑤ **LAWSON MCGHEE LIBRARY**, at 500 Church Ave., is a 1971 modernist work by Bruce McCarty. It's the third library to honor the memory of the daughter of railroad-industry tycoon Charles McClung McGhee. Lawson McGhee died in childbirth in 1883.

⑥ ⑦ The **YMCA** and **YWCA**, both on Clinch Avenue, are both historic. The YW was dedicated in 1925, and has been a residential refuge for women in need since its earliest days. Its lobby was used as a shooting locale for the 1999 Jake Gyllenhaal movie *October Sky*, in which it stood in for the lobby of an Indianapolis hotel.

LAWSON MCGHEE LIBRARY

Although in a modern building, **LAWSON MCGHEE** *is the* **OLDEST PUBLIC LIBRARY** *in* **TENNESSEE**

JAMES PARK HOUSE

Further west along Clinch, the YMCA, designed by the distinctively romantic mind of Charles Barber, still has athletic facilities, but its residential floors are now private condos. It was once popular as a residence for men involved in the conservationist movement, including Benton MacKaye, the creator of the Appalachian Trail, who lived here for a short time in the '30s, and Ernie Dickerman, who lived here for many years as he became a nationally prominent conservationist. In 1944, the FBI captured a Nazi spy here; the German immigrant had been inquiring into work at Oak Ridge.

GAY STREET

One of Knoxville's original streets, Gay Street earned the distinction of one of "America's Great Places" by the American Planning Association in 2012. It was the site of both the founding of the University of Tennessee (as Blount College, in 1794), and the state of Tennessee, founded by a constitutional convention believed to have taken place at the southwest corner of Gay and Church, in 1796.

It connects on one end to the Gay Street Bridge, the 1898 steel bridge over the Tennessee River. Built for pedestrians and horses, it turned out to be plenty sturdy for automobile traffic. However, no use has been more famous than that of Harvey Logan, a.k.a. Kid Curry, the Wild-West outlaw who rode the sheriff's stolen horse across this bridge in June, 1903, never to be seen again. It's the setting of several scenes in the Cormac McCarthy novel, *Suttree*, set in 1951, including a suicide.

Gay Street's name, taken for granted by generations of Knoxvillians but often startling to new-comers, honors an older street in Baltimore, a city much admired at the time of Knoxville's founding. It became Knoxville's main commercial street, but also its mainstream entertainment district. Today, it's only half-jokingly called Knoxville's "theater district." Gay Street's theaters have made it a natural focus for 21st century festivals, like Big Ears and Rossini.

1854 | Knoxville became AMERICA'S THIRD CITY *to open a* YMCA

LAMAR HOUSE, 1876

Bijou Theatre & Lamar House

Located at 803 South Gay Street
865-522-0832 • *knoxbijou.org*
BOX OFFICE MON–FRI: 10AM–5PM
SAT: 10AM–2PM *or 1 hr before a show*

The Bijou Theatre is the region's oldest surviving theater, a 1909 vaudeville house—but it's really two historic buildings, as the front of the theater, including the lobby, box office, and adjacent restaurant, are located in a much-older building, a ca. 1817 hotel known as the Lamar House.

Clad in stuccoed brick, the Lamar House is Knoxville's oldest commercial building, and connects to Andrew Jackson's early career. It hosted a fete in his honor, when Young Hickory was known mainly as the hero of the Battle of New Orleans. The Lamar included a barber shop, ballroom, confectionary, and a popular saloon, which witnessed Civil War-era political arguments and occasional gunfights.

During that war, the hotel included a temporary office for Confederate Gen. Joseph Johnston, and also hosted balls enjoyed by rebel spy Belle Boyd. Later in the same year, controlled by the Union army, it was where Gen. William Sanders was brought after sustaining mortal wounds on the battlefield. He died here, attended by Gen. Burnside himself. Fearing a crisis in morale when Union forces were under siege, Burnside chose to withhold the news of the popular young commander's death, having him buried secretly at midnight.

Six years after the war, former Confederate Gen. James Clanton of Alabama was carried here after he was mortally wounded in a gunfight with a former Union officer on Gay Street. He became the second Civil War general to die in this building.

The **LAMAR HOUSE** *was the* **FINEST HOTEL** *in the Knoxville area during the Civil War*

The hotel was no longer Knoxville's finest when it became the entrance to the Bijou Theatre in early 1909. The Bijou holds 750, though in its early heyday it held twice as many, with narrower seats, fewer fire standards, and a second balcony, usually reserved for black patrons, now off limits.

The Bijou has witnessed a pageant of American show business: the Marx Brothers (15 years before their movie career!), John Philip Sousa, Pavlova, Blackstone, Eddie Cantor, Will Rogers, Sophie Tucker, all during the early vaudeville era. Then the theater took a turn as a dramatic stage, presenting Tallulah Bankhead, Sidney Greenstreet, Montgomery Clift, as well as local stars like future Tony winner John Cullum.

In decline by the '60s, the Bijou did nine years as a porno-movie theater, and was almost torn down before its preservationist revival in 1974. Since then, it has hosted a wide variety of shows, from Dizzy Gillespie to the Ramones.

BISTRO AT THE BIJOU OCCUPIES THE SPACE OF A PRE-CIVIL WAR SALOON

POSTERS AND PHOTOGRAPHS OF BIJOU THEATRE PERFORMERS LINE THE WALLS OF THE BISTRO

Then, after a substantial renovation and serving as a venue for the internationally prominent Big Ears Festival, it unexpectedly received national acclaim. The Bijou was about a century old when a *New York Times* critic declared its acoustics to be among the finest of any theater in the nation.

In the same building, the Bistro at the Bijou occupies a historic place originally occupied by the pre-Civil War Lamar House Saloon. After serving many other purposes (including, by 1932, Knoxville's first Chinese restaurant, the Pagoda), it opened as the Bistro in 1980, and is among Knoxville's most historic restaurant spaces. Known for its creative menu and live jazz, its latter-day patrons have included Cormac McCarthy and Doc Watson.

Across the street from the Bijou, the corner of Gay and Cumberland once hosted a cluster of theaters, the oldest and largest of which was Staub's Opera House, an elaborate European-style auditorium built by Swiss immigrant (and Knoxville mayor) Peter Staub, in 1872. Later known as the Lyric, it was torn down in 1956. Look for the historical marker on the wall.

ORNATE SEATING BOXES WITH CHERUBS THAT WERE PART OF THE ORIGINAL 1909 DESIGN

Built in 1909, the BIJOU *still hosts over* 100 SHOWS A YEAR

THE TENNESSEE THEATRE ON THE DAY IT OPENED IN OCTOBER 1928

TENNESSEE THEATRE: A GRAND ENTERTAINMENT PALACE

 Tennessee Theatre

Located at 604 South Gay Street
865-684-1200 • *tennesseetheatre.com*
BOX OFFICE MON-FRI: 10AM–5PM
SAT: 10AM–2PM *or 1 hr before a show*

Extraordinary among medium-sized cities, Knoxville boasts two restored historic theaters. Just two blocks down the street from the Bijou is the Tennessee Theatre, the 1928 motion-picture palace reborn as a performing-arts center. The extravagant Moorish Revival theatre, with its original Mighty Wurlitzer organ, is a rare survivor of the brief "motion-picture palace" era, and its broad, transverse oval shape may make it unique.

In its early days, the Tennessee combined movies with big shows starring cowboy star Tom Mix (and his horse, Tony, as part of a rodeo-acrobatic act!); jazz bandleader Glenn Miller; and young Cuban heartthrob Desi Arnaz.

In 1935, Ziegfeld's Follies, starring Fanny Brice, drew perhaps the biggest crowd in the theater's history. The Tennessee rarely featured country music, but it was the site of local fiddler Roy Acuff's first auditorium performance, at a 1931 talent show.

The movie palace hosted several "world premiere" events in the 1950s and '60s, drawing real-life stars like Tony Perkins, Merv Griffin—and Robert Preston, star of the Agee-based film, *All the Way Home*, in 1963.

It closed as a cinema in 1977, but opened for occasional special events, and by the 1980s was hosting jazz, rock, pop, and symphony shows. A massive 2005 renovation, involving a cantilevered expansion of the backstage, made room for major Broadway shows and operas.

In its new guise, it has welcomed a variety of performers from Bob Dylan, Lionel Hampton, and Diana Ross to keyboardist-composer Philip Glass.

The Tennessee has shown thousands of movies and appeared in a couple. It has a brief cameo in the 1999 Jake Gyllenhaal film *October Sky* (because the scene was set in Indiana, the set designers had to alter the Tennessee's sign) and a longer scene in the 2018 Burt Reynolds movie, *The Last Movie Star*, in which its lobby serves as the lobby of a posh hotel.

Also within Gay Street's theater theme is the eight-screen cineplex known as the Regal Riviera—a new theater from 2007 whose name honors the large 1920 Riviera theater that attracted audiences to the same spot for more than half a century.

1937 | About 70,000 PEOPLE *watched* SNOW WHITE *during one week at the Tennessee*

10 Andrew Johnson Hotel

Located at 912 South Gay Street

Right by the Gay Street Bridge, the Andrew Johnson Hotel was the tallest building in East Tennessee at the time of its completion in 1929. Knoxville's largest and most luxurious hotel opened just in time to receive the first Smokies national-park visitors.

THE ANDREW JOHNSON HOTEL, ONCE EAST TENNESSEE'S TALLEST BUILDING

Now an office building, the Andrew Johnson served as a hotel for almost half a century, and its guests include a pageant of American and world history: Jean-Paul Sartre (who wrote a piece about American cities for *Le Figaro* here with a wartime press junket in 1945); Duke Ellington; Amelia Earhart (who stayed here in 1936, the year before her disappearance, on a solo driving trip through the Smokies, and gave a press conference in her room); King Hussein of Jordan; Sergei Rachmaninoff, who stayed here in 1943, after the final concert of his career; and playwright Tennessee Williams, who stayed here for several days in 1957, for the funeral of his father.

Most famously, it was here that singer-songwriter Hank Williams spent some of the last hours of his life, on New Year's Eve, 1952. Here he had a meal, perhaps some moonshine, and at least one shot of morphine. What happened that night has been the subject of decades of research and speculation into the reason 29-year-old Williams was found to be dead in the back of the car that left this hotel a few hours earlier. Contemporary accounts claim he was unconscious when he left the hotel, and some biographers have suggested that he died here.

Other accounts claim he was still alive, though the morphine injection he received here was likely to have played a role in his death. The location of his final hours is interesting, considering that his youthful idol was Roy Acuff—who was becoming a popular sensation in 1935–36, when he was broadcasting well-attended WNOX radio shows from the roof.

PLAZA TOWER

11 Near the Andrew Johnson is the **PLAZA TOWER** (800 S. Gay), completed in 1978 and still the tallest building in East Tennessee. It was once the headquarters of the United American Bank, run by gubernatorial contender Jake Butcher, who financed the 1982 World's Fair. The building became a center of national attention in 1983, when the bank collapsed and Butcher was arrested for bank fraud.

12 The elegantly marbled **JOURNAL ARCADE BUILDING** (618 S. Gay) was once the headquarters of the daily *Journal*; at the time of its opening in 1924, its editor was elderly Union veteran William

Since 1908, **EAST TENNESSEE'S TALLEST BUILDINGS** *have been on Gay Street*

A VIEW NORTH ON GAY ST, CA. 1930, SHOWS THE HOLSTON BUILDING ON LEFT, AND ON THE RIGHT, THE FARRAGUT, BURWELL (WITH THE TENNESSEE THEATRE), MECHANICS BANK, AND ARCADE BUILDINGS

Rule. Among those who worked here were future Pulitzer-winning war correspondent Don Whitehead and Pattie Boyd, the area's first female full-time journalist.

Farragut Hotel / Hyatt Place

Located at 530 South Gay Street

The Farragut Hotel dates to 1919, though it spent many years as an office building before it reopened as Hyatt Place in 2018. It was during the Roaring '20s Knoxville's finest hotel, and the birthplace of the Knoxville Symphony; in the old ballroom Cincinnati-born violinist Bertha Walburn Clark conducted her Little Symphony, which had grown by 1935 to become a full orchestra.

The hotel also hosted some of the meetings that led to the creation of the Great Smoky Mountains National Park. And it was here, in 1932, that the athletic powerhouse known as the Southeastern Conference was born, after days of passionate arguments among members of the unwieldy Southern Conference.

Among the Farragut's notable guests are Babe Ruth and Lou Gehrig (here in 1934, with the rest of the Yankees, for a series of exhibition games); Merv Griffin (who complained about the heat); David Ben Gurion, here to promote his favorite project, Israel; South Vietnam President Ngo Dinh Diem (here to behold TVA with Tran Van Don, one of the generals behind his overthrow and assassination six years later.)

The Farragut was one of Knoxville's earliest hotels to desegregate, and by the late '60s, James Brown launched his local radio station, WJBE, in the basement.

The FARRAGUT *may be the* SOUTH'S LARGEST BUILDING *named for a* UNION COMMANDER

14 The **MECHANICS BANK & TRUST BUILDING** (612 S. Gay St.) was the site of the Mabry-O'Conner gunfight of 1882, which not only had as high a body count as the gunfight at the O.K. Corral, the previous year, but was even more remarkable in that all three potential assailants were killed almost simultaneously. It earned national attention, and Mark Twain, who was then finishing up his most famous book of nonfiction, *Life on the Mississippi*, included a sardonic account of it. (It's an extended footnote in Chapter 40.)

Later, the fifth floor of the same building was headquarters of WROL radio, and location for early broadcasts of Flatt and Scruggs and the Everly Brothers, as well as the site of East Tennessee's first television broadcasts, in 1953.

15 The 400 block includes the 1905 **MILLER'S DEPARTMENT STORE** building, which after almost 70 years as a regionally famous retailer spent 20-odd years in hiding, when it was covered with faux-modernist mirrored glass—then to be treated to a comprehensive restoration to greet a new century as an upscale office building.

MILLER'S BUILDING CARYATID

The east side of the 400 block was the setting of the worst fire in Knoxville history, a late-night hotel fire in 1897 that spread rapidly and killed at least four. The two buildings that survived the fire were the

16 **TAILOR LOFTS BUILDING**, at the corner—dating to the 1870s, it's the block's oldest building—and the larger, more elaborate Richardsonian Romanesque

17 **CENTURY BUILDING**, to the north of Wall Avenue. Everything in between was destroyed. Reflecting the booming economy of the time, the buildings there today were built rapidly in 1897–98, generally larger than the originals.

18 Among them is the tall **PHOENIX BUILDING**, whose original name reflects the post-fire revival.

"THE GREAT GAY STREET FIRE" BY RUSSELL BRISCOE

The 400 block's **POST-FIRE BUILDINGS** *are mostly larger but less ornate than their predecessors*

THE SCENE OF THE FATAL THREE-WAY SHOOT-OUT ON GAY ST IN 1882 – THE MECHANICS BANK BUILDING, PHOTOGRAPHED IN 1923, SOON AFTER A CLASSICAL FAÇADE IMPROVEMENT

DOWNTOWN

THE FIRE OF 1897, AND EVENTUALLY OTHER FIRES, NOTABLY A DYNAMITE-EXPLOSION FIRE IN 1904, WERE EVENTUALLY BLAMED ON AN ANGRY SPIRIT, THE GHOST OF A "WHITE MULE," WHO HAD DIED ON THE SPOT DURING AN ITINERANT CIRCUS IN THE 1860S. A RURAL BELIEF HELD THAT THE SPOT WHERE A WHITE MULE DIES IS FOREVER CURSED. PRINT DESIGNED BY MARY WORKMAN

The CIRCUS *once set up on a flood plain known as* "THE OLD BASE BALL GROUNDS"

① The **EAST TENNESSEE HISTORY CENTER** is the home of the Museum of East Tennessee History and the East Tennessee Historical Society, Knox County Archives—and the McClung Collection, a regionally impressive reference library of local history and genealogy *(see p.37)*. Although the Gay Street extension, including the main entrance, is of recent vintage, the Market Street side of the building is historic. Designed by Washington architect Alfred Mullett (he designed a similar one still prominent in New Orleans), and clad in local marble, it was Knoxville's post-office building from its completion in 1874 until 1934. Its original entrance, on the Market Street side, no longer open, shows its historical relevance; its stone steps are worn down by decades of shoe leather. The McClung Collection's space includes what may be Knoxville's most beautiful secular space: the reading

THE FORMER DOWNTOWN POST OFFICE CONTAINS THE EAST TENNESSEE HISTORY CENTER WHICH FACES MARKET ST, AN EXTENSION AND ENTRANCE TO THE BUILDING IS NOW ON GAY ST

room is the old federal courtroom. It was here that outlaw Kid Curry faced federal charges in 1902 and 1903—when, apparently tiring of the ordeal, he escaped from the Knox County Jail, never to be seen alive again. The offices of Justice Edward Terry Sanford were here until he was exalted to the U.S. Supreme Court in 1923.

⑲ Next door, the **HOLSTON BUILDING**, built in 1912, was once Knoxville's tallest building. A bank and office building, it hosted the FBI during the era when bootlegging was a concern, and in the 1940s, the studios of WROL, when Tennessee Ernie Ford was an announcer, and some of the first popular bluegrass bands were getting their starts here. Flatt & Scruggs in fact made their first recordings here in 1948. It was an under-occupied office building until 2007, when maverick developer David Dewhirst, a former aerospace engineer, led a team that redeveloped it into upscale condominiums.

⑳ Across the street, adjacent to the Farragut Hotel, the **S & W CAFETERIA**, at 516 S. Gay St., is now the location of an Aveda beauty school. The once-elegant 1937 cafeteria occupied four floors of the building, including a basement and mezzanine. The cafeteria closed in 1981, but much of the building, including the brass spiral staircase, is intact.

MUSIC HISTORY EXHIBIT AT THE MUSEUM OF EAST TENNESSEE HISTORY

Many of downtown's **OLDER BUILDINGS** *are faced with* **LOCALLY QUARRIED TENNESSEE MARBLE**

THE 100 BLOCK

North of Summit Hill Drive, the 100 block of Gay is unique in Knoxville, the block affected by the city's 1919 effort to complete the original Gay Street Viaduct, by bringing the street level up to that of a new viaduct over the railroad yards. Lower levels were permanently covered, as businesses began using their second floors as first floors. Fanciful legends of what exists in "Underground Gay Street" have proliferated. However, the street is built on solid fill. Only the corridors beneath the sidewalks offer subtle remnants of the pre-1919 era.

21 The **REBORI BUILDING** at 128 S. Gay Street, served as the original Lawson McGhee Library. The building, built in 1885, housed for 30 years the region's first durable public library. Italian street vendor Fiorenzo Rebori, who'd been selling peanuts from a lean-to shack alongside the building for decades, obtained the building in a 1915 auction, hence its modern name. Owning the building, he preferred to rent it out, and kept selling peanuts from his shack.

22 Built in 1925, the **STERCHI BUILDING**, the block's only building built after the viaduct, was once the headquarters of large furniture chain Sterchi

REBORI BUILDING

STERCHI BROTHERS AND COMMERCE BUILDINGS

Bros and played a role in the growth of country music.

Across the street, the former Harold's Deli, (at 131. S. Gay Street and now Knox Mason) run by Harold Shersky for 57 years, was a rare Kosher deli with a country music heritage, frequented by the likes of Flatt & Scruggs when they were performing across the street at the old WNOX radio station. Nearby at the Three Feathers Café (at 101 S. Gay St, now Nouveau Classics), songwriter and performer Arthur Q. Smith famously sold songs for a few dollars or to clear his bar bill.

The ca. 1900 Emporium Building, at 100 S. Gay, was once a large, stylish retail space. Now an arts center, with galleries, studio, and headquarters of the symphony and several other arts organizations, it's packed with hundreds of art lovers and monthly gallery nights.

Learn more about Knoxville's musical legends on the Cradle of Country Music Tour—a self-directed walking tour around downtown. Pick up a free brochure and map ★ at the **KNOXVILLE VISITORS CENTER** near here at 301 S. Gay Street (*see p.87*).

Rounding out the "theater-district" theme, still another theater down the street is the WDVX studio, within the Visitors Center,

STERCHI BROS *promoted* PHONOGRAPHS, *and also the* MUSICIANS *who recorded records to play on them*

THE CHEROKEE MOTOR COMPANY OCCUPIED THE CAL JOHNSON BUILDING AT 301 STATE ST, CA. 1920S

which hosts live radio shows six days a week at noon. And tiny Theatre Knoxville Downtown, at 321 North Gay, a former 1950s live-radio studio, features manic and often ribald live comedy and drama. This was the site of WIVK radio, where in 1958, a 12-year-old Dolly Parton began performing on live radio before a studio audience.

STATE STREET

At 301 State Street, not far from Summit Hill, is a Victorian building different from all others in the region, for one detail: It was built and owned by a man who was raised to be a slave. His name is inscribed in marble on the third floor of the front facade:

23 CALVIN F. JOHNSON, 1898.

Despite emancipation, few former slaves had successful careers in the segregated South. Johnson, who owned real estate, built buildings, and became wealthy enough to be a significant philanthropist, broke all the rules and exceeded all expectations. Although he was best known for his chain of saloons and his horse-racing track, this building—the only one of several still standing—was originally a clothing factory, and later a car dealership.

CAL JOHNSON, *slave turned* BUSINESSMAN-PHILANTHROPIST, *was a rarity in* 19th-century America

THE MARKET HOUSE, BUILT IN 1897

MARKET SQUARE & VICINITY

Perhaps Knoxville's most durable attraction is Market Square. Established as a farmers' market in 1854 by developers Joseph Mabry and William Swan, it has served that purpose ever since—but from its early days it was much more, a cultural center, the very heart of the city and even the greater region. Farm produce has always been its defining principle, and today on Saturday and Wednesday market days during the growing season (May to November), it draws thousands. But it has also seen riots, concerts, demonstrations, celebrations, and nearly every sort of business. It has attracted musicians and novelists and national politicians. It hosted the Women's Christian Temperance Union's regional headquarters, as well as about seven saloons.

It was well-known by the time of the Civil War, when its small city-owned market house was loaded with Union ammunition, causing anxiety in town and a formal complaint from the Unionist mayor. By 1870 it was flanked by two rows of brick buildings, giving it the general look we know today. The city built a tall, slim, elaborate Market Hall in the center of the square in 1897; it was torn down in 1960, replaced with a modernist design for a "mall"—later replaced, itself, beginning in the 1980s, with approaches that respected the surviving Victorian designs.

The Market Hall's auditorium drew crowds to see Duke Ellington, Roy Acuff, Booker T. Washington, Carrie Nation, William Jennings Bryan. Ronald Reagan spoke in the open square in 1980. Suffragists, Republicans, and Socialists have held rallies here. Once home of the seat of city government, it was here that the region's first black elected officials, city aldermen in 1869, attended public meetings.

MARKET SQUARE *once hosted both* UNION *and* CONFEDERATE VETERANS' HALLS

The setting has captured the attention of several novelists, notably Cormac McCarthy, who describes Market Square extensively in two novels, *The Orchard Keeper* and *Suttree*; James Agee, who sets two scenes here in *A Death in the Family*; and David Madden, who makes it a scene in *Bijou*. Market Square also appears in the work of Anne Armstrong, Rick Yancey, and others.

Most of Market Square's buildings date from about 1865 to 1910. Of special interest is ㉔ the **PETER KERN BUILDING** at the southwest corner. One of the earliest works of influential local architect Joseph Baumann, it was built in 1876 for German-immigrant baker and later mayor Peter Kern. Not only a bakery and candy factory, it was an emporium of delights, featuring a soda fountain, toy store, "ice-cream saloon," and ballroom. It's now occupied by the Oliver Hotel, two ground-floor restaurants, and a "speakeasy" known as Peter Kern's Library (his portrait is behind the bar).

Note that all of Market Square's addresses are one- and two-digit numbers, and that they advance in opposite order from the rest of downtown. When the city standardized addresses in the early 1890s, Market Square was the only part of town allowed to retain its original, mid-19th century addressing system.

KERN BUILDING

TENNESSEE WOMAN SUFFRAGE MEMORIAL

The large bronze bell on the south end of the square once hung in the tower of the City Hall, at the other end of the Market House, and sounded alarms, in the pre-radio era,

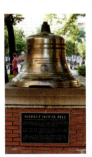

MARKET HOUSE BELL

about local crises, like riots or fires. Removed as a safety hazard long before its building was torn down, it traveled around the region, serving various purposes outside of downtown (during World War II it signaled blackout drills in East Knoxville) before its return to Market Square as a permanent symbol in the 1980s. The ➓ **SUFFRAGE STATUE**, representing the role of Tennessee feminists in the national suffrage movement, was installed in 2006. The woman in the middle, the youngest of the trio, is Knoxville's own Lizzie Crozier French, a single mother who as early as the 1880s was here on the square exhorting crowds to support the vote for women. She lived to see it happen, and died in 1926 as an elderly political activist still at work in Washington.

PETER KERN *was one of many* GERMAN REFUGEES *of the Revolutions of* 1848

One episode in the summer of 1954 says a lot about the diverse crowds that formed in Market Square every day. At the time, a music scout for RCA had a theory that a record store on Market Square was a dependable test market for the entire nation. That summer, one 78 by an unknown truck driver from Memphis was becoming a sensation on Market Square, among black, white, young, and old. Store owner Sam Morrison was playing from speakers on the square, a disk cut by Memphis' Sun Records called "That's All Right" by Elvis Presley. The scout bought a copy for himself, and one for the president of the company. RCA bought out Presley's contract the following year for a huge sum and never looked back. This story is part of Knoxville's Cradle of Country Music Tour.

Also in the Market Square area, Union Avenue includes the companion buildings the **PEMBROKE** (originally known as the New Sprankle) and the **DAYLIGHT**, now home to Union Ave. Books, and other businesses. The taller building was for more than 40 years the main headquarters for TVA, 1933–76, in its most active, world-famous era, when it was building multiple dams in Tennessee, Alabama, and Kentucky, and drawing international

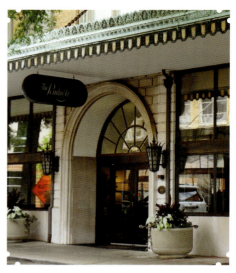

THE PEMBROKE

attention. The Daylight also included engineering offices. When visitors like Nehru, prime minister of India and Le Corbusier, the noted Swiss architect, visited Knoxville to see TVA's wonders, they stopped in here. In the early 1980s, the Pembroke was one of Knoxville's first preservationist-era residential projects—along with nearby Kendrick Place, the circa 1910 townhouse development on Locust Street.

The **MASONIC TEMPLE**, also on Locust Street, has looked as it does now for well over half a century. But it's actually a radical remodeling of a delicately adorned Victorian mansion of Charles McClung McGhee, railroad tycoon and donor of the first Lawson McGhee Library.

THE OLD CITY

Though little more than an intersection and its associated blocks, the Old City is a late 19th century commercial district, known in recent decades for restaurants, off-beat shops, and live-music nightclubs.

THE DAYLIGHT BUILDING

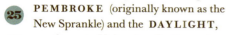

Long neglected, the **DAYLIGHT BUILDING** was once targeted for demolition

JFG COFFEE AND JACKSON ATELIERS BUILDINGS ON W JACKSON AVE

DOWNTOWN

Its name is, to begin with, a bit of a misnomer. The Old City is not the original or oldest part of town. To the contrary, its streets weren't fully laid out until 1888; previously, an architectural-lumber factory had sprawled across the site. Jackson, a railroad-frontage street, sprang up suddenly, bisecting that old factory acreage, supporting sometimes grandiose wholesale warehouse construction—as Central, a very different street, grew small buildings, saloons, secondhand shops, drugstores, boarding houses, pool halls and bordellos, stretching to the river wharf. The area boomed with grocery, garment, and packing industries, some of it declining by the mid-20th century. By the 1970s, the phrase "Old City" was a popular way to refer to a long-neglected corner of the city that seemed a Victorian neighborhood preserved in amber, never threatened by new development and overlooked by urban renewal—which had erased almost everything to its east and south.

What had survived was not one neighborhood but the intersection of several old neighborhoods—pocket grocery, garment, and meatpacking districts; the saloon district known as the Bowery; a predominantly black residential district known as Cripple Creek; and a bit of Irish Town. All they had in common was their proximity to the railroad.

The corner of Jackson and Central became ground zero for numbering all the addresses in the entire county. Hence, and sometimes confusingly, most of the addresses in the Old City, going in all four directions, begin with 1.

Speculators were working on these challenging old buildings by the mid-1970s, but it wasn't until 1983, when a restaurant-nightclub known as Annie's—run by Annie DeLisle, ex-wife of novelist Cormac McCarthy—that the place started to show obvious signs of new life.

The once-swampy **OLD CITY** *area attracted* **FISHERMEN**, *ca. 1800-1850*

65

ICON OF THE BOWERY AND THE OLD CITY, THE FORMER PATRICK SULLIVAN'S SALOON

 ## 28 *Patrick Sullivan's Saloon*

Located at 100 North Central Street
865-999-5251 • *lonesomedove
knoxville.com* • MON-THURS: 4:30-10PM
FRI: 11:30AM-2:30PM & 4:30-11PM
SAT: 4:30-11PM

The Old City's conspicuous anchor is Patrick Sullivan's Saloon, currently Lonesome Dove bistro at 100 N. Central Street. Built in 1888 by Irish immigrant Sullivan, near the site of his previous saloon, it was a landmark in its own day, and unusual in that it permitted everybody, including women, banned from most American saloons of the day, and blacks. One of Sullivan's partners was Dan Dewine, who had run brewpubs in the area. Dewine did so well in the saloon business that he bought real estate on the north side of town, and, in the 1920s, enabled the establishment of St. Mary's, East Tennessee's first Catholic hospital.

After the city banned saloons in 1907, the building supported the Armetta family, Sicilian immigrants who lived and made ice cream here, for which they became famous. The Armetta name is still barely legible in white paint on the brick.

The building's round brick window was adopted as a symbol of the Old City, and repeated in a few other buildings, like Java—which opened in 1991, before Knoxville's first Starbucks, and has operated under that name, through several different managements, since then.

 A plainer building notable for its clerestory skylight, **BOYD'S JIG & REEL** was originally a Bowery-era (ca. 1890s) drugstore, back when several drugs now strictly controlled, like cocaine and morphine, were freely available over the counter. For many years beginning in the 1920s, it was a Greek-run chili parlor and bar called the Manhattan Cafe, notable for the fact it had equal-sized parallel rooms for blacks and whites. Stick McGhee, the bluesman who later wrote one of the first rock'n'roll hits, "Drinkin' Wine, Spo-dee-o-dee" worked here as a waiter in the early '40s. The Manhattan name was revived during the preservation era, when it reopened as Manhattan's in 1987, hosting numerous jazz,

IMMIGRANTS *from* IRELAND, ITALY, GREECE, *and* RUSSIA *were once obvious on Central*

folk, and rock bands. It became the Scottish-themed Boyd's Jig and Reel in 2011.

Several Old City clubs have hosted nationally significant performers, but none more than the legendary basement club Ella Guru, at 111 N. Central. During its short tenure, ca. 1988–90, it welcomed an incredible array of folk, blues, jazz, country, and experimental musicians, from Brian Eno to Sun Ra. Garth Brooks, who performed there before he was famous, referred to the memorable place by name in his 1995 autobiographical barnburner, "The Old Stuff."

30 West Jackson Avenue includes a cluster of rare **RICHARDSONIAN ROMANESQUE BUILDINGS** of the late 1880s, exhibiting with surprising contrasts of stone, terra cotta, and different-colored brick, with extravagant ornamentation (look for the angry satyrs!). The depression of 1893 put an end to this expensive style.

Remnants of old advertising can be seen on the buildings including Haynes-Henson, shoe distributors.

31 **JFG FLATS**, an apartment building, is in an old coffee-roasting factory. It was the third and longest location of the popular Southern brand. JFG moved into the building in the 1930s; it was previously the Bowman Hat Factory, which had moved to what became known as Homberg Place in Bearden, for one of their products.

LOOKING WEST ALONG W JACKSON AVE

Jackson, west of Gay, is a recently reviving neighborhood, once known for light industry and the vast C.M. McClung warehouses, the center of that major mail-order hardware business. They were being considered for renovation when they burned in two spectacular fires in the early 21st century. The Standard, a popular event space, was a near-ruined former glass factory until developer David Dewhirst and architect Mark Heinz saw new potential for it. Likewise, the Southeastern Glass building, taller than it looks, was imaginatively redeveloped as a residential building by Sanders Pace Architecture.

Summit Hill Drive covers the course of Vine Street, the black community's major artery, known for its movie theaters, drugstores, barber shops, and black-run hotels. In her short memoir, "400 Mulvaney Street," Nikki Giovanni recalls Vine Street in the '40s and '50s with fondness.

Blacks and whites mixed along S. Central more than elsewhere in town, generally peacefully, with the major exception of Labor Day weekend, 1919. A riot that began with a frustrated white lynch mob, unable to get to a black man arrested for murdering a white woman, surged into this neighborhood, as state guardsmen, called in to quell the white rioters, joined them in besieging the black community, training machine guns along Central. Although the official death toll of the riot was only two, it's long been rumored that many more died that night.

RICHARDSONIAN ROMANESQUE BUILDINGS ON W JACKSON AVE

JACKSON'S OLDER BUILDINGS were built suddenly, ca. 1888-1893

LOOKING NORTH TOWARDS THE RESTORED WHITE LILY FLATS BUILDING ON NORTH CENTRAL ST

32 The large building on North Central known as **WHITE LILY FLATS** is actually slightly older than all the buildings along Central and Jackson. Built in 1885 by J. Allen Smith, a newcomer from Atlanta, it was, for 120 years, the factory where White Lily Flour was made. Though best known in the South, its international trade included Cuba. White Lily moved its operations to the Midwest in 2006, and its old mill became a popular apartment building.

Depot Street was, for 115 years, the first street railroad passengers saw upon disembarking in Knoxville. East Tennessee's first railroad arrived along here on July 4, 1855. A previous station was accompanied by a small railroad hotel, which was the site of pioneer American humorist George Washington Harris's mysterious death in 1869.

The Knoxville-based East Tennessee, Virginia, and Georgia Railroad, which connected much of the South, was based here from 1869 to 1894, when J.P. Morgan purchased it as a major component of his new Southern Railway. In 1897, this street was central to the "Battle of Depot Street," a fatal riot among hundreds of streetcar construction workers that resulted from William Gibbs McAdoo's unsanctioned attempt to build a new streetcar line along this street.

THE SOUTHERN RAILWAY STATION, BUILT IN 1903

WHITE LILY *is demanded in some* CAKE *and* BISCUIT RECIPES

SOUTHERN RAILWAY STATION

Located at 306 West Depot Avenue
865-249-7808 • southernstationtn.com
MON–THURS: 11AM–7PM
FRI–SAT: 11AM–8PM • SUN: NOON–5PM

THREE RIVERS RAMBLER EMBARKS FROM UNIVERSITY COMMONS DEPOT

The old Southern Railway station, finished in 1903, is now an office building with a winery and event space. Designed by Frank Pierce Milburn, it was notable for its symmetrical design, which balanced the white and black sections, interpreting the new "separate but equal" standard literally. It originally included a tall clock tower, removed as a hazard in 1945.

The station was part of the story of the worst transportation disaster in regional history, the New Market Wreck in 1904, which was a collision, 20 miles east of Knoxville, between a train that had just left this station and another whose passengers were expecting to get off here. Some 70 people were killed, and many more seriously injured.

THE CABOOSE AT THE OLD SMOKY RAILWAY MUSEUM AT THE SOUTHERN STATION

The wreck became the subject of ballads, especially one that was often sung at this station by a particular guitarist and songwriter named Charlie Oaks, a blind minstrel who played for tips and sometimes sold copies of his lyrics. Years later, he made a few commercial records. Some historians have proposed that Oaks was the first professional country musician.

The station was open 24 hours a day, and greeted millions of passengers in its history. A few of them were famous, ranging from Presidents Wilson and Taft, Buffalo Bill, Tallulah Bankhead, and Al Jolson. The funeral train of William Jennings Bryan stopped here in 1925.

The last regular passenger train to stop here was a night train from Birmingham to Washington in 1970.

Housed at the Southern Railway Station is the Old Smoky Railway Museum, featuring historic passenger railway cars, Pullman coaches, a U.S. Mail car, and a caboose. The museum is adjacent to the active Norfolk Southern freight yard.

Depot and Gay once formed a cluster of large hotels catering to the railroad-passenger crowd. Only part of one remains, the lower two floors of the Watauga, which for 90-odd years housed the Regas Restaurant, founded by Greek immigrants in 1919. Regas Square, a new development, is named in their honor. Their old restaurant space is now a nonprofit center. The defunct Watauga's residential floors were removed from the top of Regas in the 1960s.

For an active railroad experience, the **THREE RIVERS RAMBLER** runs excursions during the autumn, with seasonal specials including Christmas runs, from the depot at University Commons at 2560 University Commons Way.

The **SOUTHERN STATION** *once welcomed* 30 **PASSENGER TRAINS** *a day*

OFF THE GRID

34 Several blocks to the northeast of Depot Street is **KNOXVILLE HIGH SCHOOL** (at 101 E. 5th Avenue), built in 1910 on a design by Baumann and Baumann, which was, for more than 40 years, the city's main high school for white children. Among its students was James Agee, who attended ca. 1924–25—it inspired a couple of his first short stories, unflattering satires of an overcrowded school. Its auditorium hosted many community productions, including early performances of the precursors to the Knoxville Symphony Orchestra, perhaps encouraging some of its students to consider show business. Actress Patricia Neal was an alumnus, and the future Oscar-winner appeared in plays here in 1940, impressing local newspaper columnists. Other show-biz alumni include Tony-winning actor John Cullum and opera singer Mary Costa. (MGM director Clarence Brown was an alum, and used a KHS banner at the beginning of his 1935 movie, *Ah, Wilderness*—but he attended in a previous building.) The Doughboy Statue out front, dedicated in 1922, is an homage to World War I dead from Knoxville, many of whom were alumni of KHS.

The steep knoll just north of Market Square is officially Summit Hill, a term which is now better known in reference to the drive that traverses the hill. It's the highest point downtown, and the location of a couple of historic institutions, including the original school for the deaf and Immaculate Conception Catholic Church. But before those were built, it originally went by another name: **GALLOWS HILL**. During

35 Knoxville's first 50 years or so, it was a place for public executions. The one best remembered may be that of a handsome young man who was hanged in 1828 for murdering his lover's husband. Because he was

KNOXVILLE HIGH SCHOOL

young and healthy at the time of his hanging, Rev. Stephen Foster, a physics professor at the university, asked the sheriff if he could borrow the corpse for a moment afterward. With that permission, Foster loaded the unfortunate onto a wagon and took him to the Second Presbyterian Church, then on Market Street near Clinch. There he had an impressive galvanic battery waiting, and he proceeded to apply electrodes to the killer's body, sometimes making it appear to revive. When Foster realized his experiment was being witnessed by a large crowd outside the church, he put the equipment away and returned the body to the family. Such experiments were common in Europe at the time, the era of Mary Shelley's *Frankenstein*, though in most cases they were conducted on animal parts.

The same steep hill that had hosted hangings got its current name of Summit Hill in the 1850s. By then, the 1851 school for the deaf and the 1855 Catholic church made the rocky crag a little less bleak. In 1863, it was the site of Union Fort Comstock, well positioned to protect both the railroad yards and Market Square. For decades, the hilltop was even a fashionable address. By the 1880s, one hillside estate included a private garden where deer grazed behind an ornate fence.

But after all this time, it's still a bit of a climb, and removed from the rest of downtown Knoxville.

*Closed since 1951, **KNOXVILLE HIGH** is now an upscale residence for elders*

BARNUM AND BAILEY ARRIVES IN TOWN WITH THE TRADITIONAL ELEPHANT PARADE DOWN GAY STREET. BY 1898, KNOXVILLE'S RAIL CONNECTIONS MADE IT A CROSSROADS FOR CIRCUSES (USUALLY SEVERAL EACH YEAR) AND MULTIPLE OTHER PUBLIC SPECTACLES.

DOWNTOWN

FIRST PRESBYTERIAN CHURCH

DOWNTOWN CHURCHES

Although a visiting Presbyterian minister in 1811 bemoaned Knoxville's lack of churches, downtown is home to several houses of worship, all of them in historic buildings—even if, in each case, it's not the congregation's original building.

1 First Presbyterian

Located at 620 State Street
865-546-2531 • *fpcknox.org*
SUN SERVICES: 8:45AM & 11AM

First Presbyterian credibly claims a founding date of 1792, when Pennsylvania-born minister Samuel Carrick was at least occasionally serving a Presbyterian congregation here. However, the church, which apparently met in public places, did not build its own edifice until 1816, having accepted James White's offer of his turnip patch for a church and graveyard. The exposed limestone boulder is part of the church's story, in that the first chapel was built upon a rock, a literal reference to Jesus's metaphor about St. Peter.

The current church building, completed in 1901, is the third on this site. Its interior is noted for its puritan simplicity, but its colorful late-Victorian stained-glass windows include a couple that were designed by Tiffany. The adjacent graveyard was here about 20 years before Knoxville's first church was built (*see p.161*).

2 First Baptist

Located at 510 West Main Street
865-546-9661 • *fbcknox.org*
SUN SERVICES: 8:45AM & 11AM

This agreeable Baroque Classical church building impressed *New Yorker* architectural critic Brendan Gill, who on a 1982 visit compared it to the work of Christopher Wren. Designed by Nashville's Dougherty and Gardner, it opened in 1924, replacing an earlier church on Gay Street. Originally its tall steeple concealed a radio tower. Knoxville's second radio station to go on air, in fact, was WFBC, a religious station based here. Its interior is especially unusual, with an exotic octagonal design. It was the home church of opera and cinema singer Mary Costa, who sang here as a child in the 1930s and '40s.

OCTAGONAL INTERIOR OF FIRST BAPTIST

An early FIRST PRESBYTERIAN ELDER *was humorist* GEORGE WASHINGTON HARRIS

ST. JOHN'S EPISCOPAL

 ## St. John's Episcopal

Located at 413 Cumberland Avenue
865-525-7347 • stjohnscathedral.org
SUN SERVICES: 8AM & 10:30AM

The second church building on this site, St. John's was designed in a Romanesque style featuring turrets, rose windows, and cruciform interior by Ohio architect J.W. Yost. It's Yost's only known work in the South. Designated the cathedral of East Tennessee's diocese, St. John's has been considerably expanded since, but the 1892 corner church is intact. Several Knoxvillians prominent in the arts were parishioners here, notably author James Agee, who was baptized here in 1910, and sang in the choir. Landscape painter, Charles Krutch, known as the "Corot of the South", often played organ here.

INTERIOR OF ST. JOHN'S EPISCOPAL

Longtime rector **THOMAS HUMES**, *onetime UT president, died as this church was being built*

Church Street Methodist

Located at 900 Henley Street
865-524-3048 • churchstreetumc.org

SUN SERVICES: 8:30AM & 11AM
WED SERVICE: NOON

Wearing its misnomer proudly, Church Street Methodist is located on Henley Street at Cumberland Avenue—but before this grand edifice rose in 1930, it was located on Church Street, and was the origin of that street's name. Perhaps Knoxville's grandest church (with only a couple of west-side Catholic churches as rivals), it was designed as a team project by local architect Charles Barber, who loved the Gothic style, and nationally prominent architect John Russell Pope, best known for his monumental work (like the Jefferson Memorial) in Washington. Its completion coincided with the opening of the Great Smoky Mountains National Park; the opening of the Henley Street Bridge, and daily stream of traffic toward the bridge may have been a motive for making a grand gesture here. Often used for non-ecclesiastical purposes, it hosted the first-ever performance of the Knoxville Symphony Orchestra in 1935. In recent years, it has been a memorable venue for music festivals.

CHURCH STREET METHODIST

Despite its **GOTHIC** *appearance,* **CHURCH STREET** *is downtown's newest church building*

5 IMMACULATE CONCEPTION

Located at 414 West Vine Avenue
865-522-1508 • *icknoxville.org*
MASS SAT: 8:30AM & 6PM • SUN: 8:30,
10, 11:30AM • MON-FRI: 12:10PM

The second iteration of East Tennessee's first Catholic church, I.C. was built in 1886, when many of its parishioners were still Irish refugees of the 1840s famine. The design by Baumann Brothers has a couple of unusual distinctions. One is that it faces away from most of downtown—but toward the train station, and Irish Town, the immigrant community now vanished where perhaps a majority of Knoxville's Catholics then lived. Another is that its four-sided clock, an addition to the original design, was sponsored by the city of Knoxville, responding to the oft-bemoaned lack of a public clock in the vicinity of Market Square and the train station.

ST. JOHN'S LUTHERAN, CA. 1930S

IMMACULATE CONCEPTION

6 ST. JOHN'S LUTHERAN

Located at 544 Broadway
865-523-3330 • *sjlcknox.org*
SUN SERVICES: 9AM & 11AM

St. John's Lutheran stands at the northern end of downtown on Broadway at Emory Place. Founded in 1888, Knoxville's first English-language Lutheran church built this stone monument in 1912 on a design by well-known local architect R.F. Graf. Its Gothic-revival style with arches, spires, and buttresses, suggests comparisons to European cathedrals, which it resembles in miniature.

1888 *Knoxville elected its* FIRST IRISH CATHOLIC MAYOR

BELA FLECK PERFORMS AT CHURCH STREET METHODIST DURING THE BIG EARS FESTIVAL IN 2018

STATUES

Early Knoxvillians, whether reflecting thrift or strict protestant interpretations of the warning about graven images, built few if any statues. The city's first statues appeared not on street corners or in public parks, but in cemeteries, and then not until after the Civil War. The late Victorian era, beginning in the 1870s, saw an almost sudden trend to erect statues as gravestone memorials. The overwhelming majority of them were statues of women, sometimes angels, most often memorializing women and girls who died young. However, a few reflected grief over the Civil War dead, like the Confederate memorial statue in Bethel Cemetery (1893), which marks a mass grave of hundreds of soldiers buried there, and the Union monument in National Cemetery (1906, replacing an earlier bronze destroyed by lightning) *(see p.164)*.

1 STATUE OF A FIREMAN

Perhaps the first public statue not in a cemetery was a memorial honoring firemen who died on the job. Installed in 1905, originally on the courthouse lawn, the statue of a fireman carrying a baby, presumably saved from a fire, was prompted by the deaths of two firemen the previous year in the catastrophic collapse of a large retail establishment on Gay Street. The statue's peculiar distinction is that it has stood in four different locations in the downtown area. Early in its career it moved from the courthouse lawn to Emory Park, at the north end of Gay Street, where there was a firehall. It moved from there to what was then City Hall Park (now the lawn of LMU's law school). Then it crossed the street to stand at a new downtown fire department building on Summit Hill, near Locust. Plans to move that fire station may mean it will move still again. A good fireman does not stay still for long.

Knoxville had **NO FIREFIGHTER DEATHS** *until 1904, when two died in the same building collapse on Gay Street*

② THE DOUGHBOY

The Doughboy Statue, a very active figure in bronze honoring Knoxville's losses in World War I stands in front of old Knoxville High School. Dedicated in 1922 by Gen. "Black Jack" Pershing himself, it became central to Memorial Day ceremonies for many years, with Gold Star mothers reading poetry in front of it.

③ SPANISH-AMERICAN WAR

On the courthouse lawn, a statue honors soldiers of the Spanish-American War. Often misperceived as an explorer or Civil War soldier, the bronze man in the broad-brimmed hat was erected by veterans themselves in a ceremony in 1940, as the world was on the brink of another war. It was, for whatever reason, the last statue erected downtown for decades.

④ VIETNAM MEMORIAL

A semi-abstract marble Vietnam memorial was cobbled together just in time for the visit of a military dignitary in 1973. It's one of a very few Vietnam monuments installed in America while the war was still on, and is therefore one of the nation's oldest. The tactically clever design by architect Arnold Schwarzbart uses three interlocking marble pieces to depict an eagle with a broken wing. It originally stood on the lawn of City Hall (now LMU), and is now on the front lawn of the City County Building.

⑤ THE OARSMAN

New construction by a private developer prompted a conceptual statue known as "The Rowboat Man," which startled pedestrians at the corner of Gay and Church in 1988. It's actually the first-ever commission by Oklahoma artist David Phelps. There's a never-disproven rumor that it represents Cormac McCarthy's antihero, Suttree, who spent a lot of time in a rowboat. Although Phelps did not name the sculpture at the time of its installation, and casually suggested to a reporter that it could be called "Hope in Adversity," he now lists it as "The Oarsman."

⑥ ALEX HALEY

The Alex Haley statue appeared in 1998 in a part of Morningside Park that became known as Haley Heritage Square, to honor the author of *Roots* who had lived in the Knoxville area in his later life. The big bronze, once the largest statue of an African-American in the world, was the work of California sculptor Tina Allen (1949–2008), commissioned to honor Haley, who had died six years earlier. Allen made it clear that she expected children to climb on the statue and sit in the storyteller's lap.

The **DOUGHBOY** *and* **SPANISH-AMERICAN WAR STATUES** *were once central to* **MEMORIAL DAY** *ceremonies*

7. BELOVED WOMAN OF JUSTICE

Audrey Flack's "Beloved Woman of Justice" appeared in the Howard Baker Federal Courthouse courtyard with the massive renovation of the Whittle Communications building to be a federal justice center. It reflects a Cherokee tradition of trusting an honored woman with special judicial powers. The sculptor, New York artist Audrey Flack (b. 1931), attended its unveiling in 2000, along with the building's honoree, former Sen. Howard Baker.

8. SERGEI RACHMANINOFF

The statue of Sergei Rachmaninoff, the only statue of the famous Russian composer in the Western Hemisphere, was the creation of obscure Russian sculptor Viktor Bokarev, but was bronzed locally and installed here in 2003 *(see p.145).*

9. ROTARY CLUB CENTENNIAL STATUE

The large bronze of a man administering a vaccine to a child honors Rotary Club leader William Sergeant (1919–2011), a longtime Oak Ridger who was a leader in the effort to eradicate polio worldwide. It was installed in 2006, when Sergeant was still alive. The Rotary Club raised money to erect the "Centennial Statue," designed by Hungarian sculptor Lajos Biro to be installed in Krutch Park, leading many to assume the honoree is Mr. Krutch—another bald, long-lived philanthropist who resembled Sergeant. Biro, who is a Rotarian himself, is prolific in Hungary, but this may be his only work in America.

10. TENNESSEE WOMAN SUFFRAGE MEMORIAL

Also in 2006, the Suffrage statue, the result of a privately funded campaign, appeared on Market Square, depicting three women who fought for the right to vote in Tennessee: Anne Dallas Dudley, Elizabeth Meriwether, and Lizzie Crozier French—the last of whom, the middle figure in the statue, was very familiar with Market Square, as a place to exhort the crowds *(see p.63).*

11. FEBB & HARRY BURN

Installed in 2018, downtown's newest statue also deals with the subject of Suffrage, depicting state legislator Harry Burn, whose vote turned a sharply divided state legislature to approve the 19th amendment, guaranteeing the right to vote for women—and thus assuring the amendment's passage nationally. The woman depicted in the statue is his mother, Febb Burn, who famously wrote a letter encouraging her son to vote for women's rights.

Perhaps to avoid trouble, **KNOXVILLE** *never installed a* **CIVIL WAR STATUE** *downtown*

12 THE VOLUNTEER

The Volunteer statue, installed on Volunteer Boulevard in 1968, has held its burning torch ever since. It was a long time coming; the design was a modification of a national statue competition in 1931 *(see p.105)*.

13 EUROPA & THE BULL

UT's Europa and the Bull startled Knoxvillians when it arrived at McClung Plaza in 1968, just weeks after the Volunteer statue was unveiled nearby. It was a limited casting of an earlier work by Swedish sculptor Carl Milles (1875–1955) *(see p.110)*.

14 GEN. ROBERT NEYLAND

A large bronze statue of Coach (and brigadier general) Robert Neyland (1892–1962) became part of a major redesign of the stadium named for him in 2010. The Vols' legendary coach looks over a neighborhood where the importance of football can't be denied; it's located on (Coach) Phillip Fulmer Way, near the intersection of Peyton Manning Pass.

15 PAT SUMMITT

A Pat Summitt statue was unveiled on Pat Summitt Plaza at UT in 2013,

Pat Summitt herself (1952–2016) was there to appreciate the honor, and appraise her own features in bronze. It was a gathering place for mourners at the time of her premature death three years later.

16 LINCOLN: THE FINAL SUMMATION

Lincoln Memorial University's campus has an original statue of Abraham Lincoln. Wayne Hyde, the Pennsylvania-based sculptor, was on hand for its 2018 unveiling of what he called "Lincoln: The Final Summation."

Lincoln probably never set foot in Knoxville, but his father lived in East Tennessee for a time, and his presidency obviously had a major effect on the city, where Unionist locals considered themselves "Lincolnites."

17 ADMIRAL FARRAGUT

A bronze statue of Admiral David Glasgow Farragut, the work of Knoxville sculptor Linda Rankin, was installed on Farragut Memorial Plaza, in front of Farragut Town Hall, in 2010 *(see p.42)*.

18 TREATY OF THE HOLSTON

An unusual marble statue depicts the July 2, 1791, Treaty of the Holston, one of several peace treaties between the George Washington administration and the Cherokee Nation, represented by 41 chiefs, including John Watts, a.k.a. Young Tassel. They all met along the riverbank somewhere in this vicinity with territorial governor William Blount and his assistants. Washington-based sculptor Raymond Kaskey designed

this monument, with a deliberately ambiguous theme, representing one chief defiantly turning his back on the proceedings. Another artisan, Malcolm Harlow, carved it, in time for its 1997 dedication as part of the city's Volunteer Landing development.

All of KNOXVILLE'S STATUES *depicting actual, specific people were installed after* 1990

LITERATURE & MUSIC

LITERATURE

Knoxville has bred several authors with followings around the world, several of whom have written in eloquent detail about their hometown.

JAMES AGEE (1909–1955) was a journalist, novelist, and screenwriter noted for *Let Us Now Praise Famous Men* (1940)  and *A Death in the Family*, the Knoxville-based autobiographical novel that won the Pulitzer Prize in 1957—and that inspired a successful Broadway play as well as movie and TV adaptations. Agee's

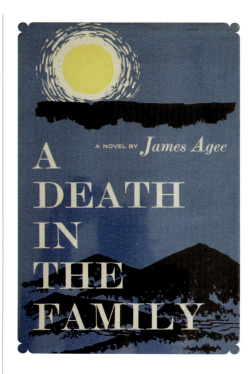

nonfiction vignette, "Knoxville: Summer 1915" was famously set to music by composer Samuel Barber. Agee was born in Knoxville and lived here for most of his youth.

NIKKI GIOVANNI (b. 1943) is a modern poet who was born in Knoxville and spent much of her childhood here. Well known for her association with the Black Power movement of the 1960s, she has written poems and short essays about her Knoxville youth, emphasizing her family and the supportive black community of the 1940s and '50s. Her early poem, "Knoxville, Tennessee," has been adapted as an illustrated

JAMES AGEE WITH HIS MOTHER LAURA TYLER AGEE, CA. 1917

1955 | JAMES AGEE *died at age 45, but has become much more famous since*

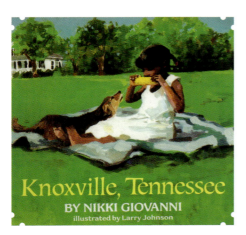

children's book. Giovanni's neighborhood was almost thoroughly erased by urban renewal in the 1960s. A historical marker notes the site of her grandmother's home.

ALEX HALEY (1921–1992), famous as the author of *Roots*, lived in Knoxville in his later years, and is honored with a large, friendly statue (see Haley Heritage Square). A familiar figure in Knoxville for 10 years, he was reportedly working on a book inspired by local settings, but it has never been discovered.

DAVID MADDEN (b. 1933) is a wide-ranging novelist and critic whose autobiographical 1974 novel, *Bijou*, about his 1940s youth in a thinly disguised Knoxville ("Cherokee") drew national attention. Although a few features are altered, Madden's recreation includes accurate descriptions of the Bijou Theatre, where he worked as a teenaged usher, and Market Square.

CORMAC MCCARTHY (b. 1933), whose work has won the Pulitzer for fiction (*The Road*) as well as a Best-Picture Oscar (*No Country for Old Men*), spent most of his first 50 years in the Knoxville area. Although he's best known for his Western themes, his early novels are set in and around his hometown, especially his first, *The Orchard Keeper* (1965), and *Suttree* (1979), which describes ca. 1951 Knoxville in unflattering but fascinating detail.

RICK YANCEY (b. 1962) is a popular young-adult novelist who stepped away from the sci-fi genre that produced *The Fifth Wave* (which became a major motion picture) to write mysteries in "The Highly Effective Detective" series (2006–2011), richly set in contemporary downtown Knoxville.

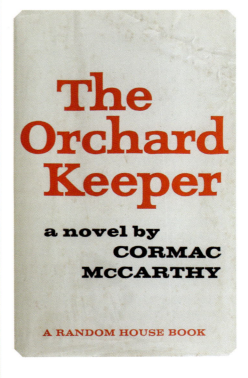

Other Knoxville authors of fiction include:

ANNE ARMSTRONG (1872–1958) was a business executive and author of two novels. The first of them, *The Seas of God* (1915), set vividly in a lightly masked version of Knoxville, called "Kingsville," was briefly an international sensation for its treatment of controversial subjects of adultery and evolution.

FRANCES HODGSON BURNETT (1849–1924) was born in England, but moved to Knoxville with her family as a teenager,

In novels, **KNOXVILLE** *has appeared by the names* **DELISLEVILLE,** **CHEROKEE,** *and* **KINGSVILLE**

Knoxville has no writers' homes to visit—almost all have vanished with the years—but some settings are still recognizable today.

THE LIFESAVER WALK
In Chapter One of *A Death in the Family*, Agee describes Rufus's walk with his father from the (long gone) Majestic Theatre on Gay Street, via Asylum Avenue (now Wall) to Market Square. From there, a walk farther west on Wall, turning right on Walnut to Summit Hill Drive, thence west on Summit Hill, would approximate their route. (Eat a Lifesaver on the way, as they did.) The "Deaf and Dumb Asylum" is the same building now occupied by LMU's law school; the L&N station he describes is well preserved as the L&N STEM academy. Beyond, following 11th Street to Highland Avenue completes the journey to the 1500 block of Highland, the setting of "Knoxville: Summer 1915."

THE CATFISH WALK
The most rewarding single walk in McCarthy's *Suttree* is early in the narrative, when the fisherman is carrying his sack of catfish and carp to sell. Begin at Volunteer Landing's riverfront, just west of Calhoun's, where Suttree's houseboat was moored. Though modern walking options don't make it easy to follow the Gay Street Bridge route Suttree took, the courthouse tower described in the book is visible. Climb the hill at Walnut and head over to Market Street, which leads to Market Square, richly described in McCarthy's passage, although the Market Hall extravagantly described ("cupoloed and crazed ... form on form in demented accretion without precedent or counterpart in the annals of architecture") was demolished in 1960—and then walk on to Gay Street (the old Arcade is gone) angling northeast down the hill toward the Old City, then the mixed-race neighborhood of "loud and shoddy commerce." (Only here does Suttree find merchants who will buy his carp.)

and began her writing career here. Although she only occasionally referred to Knoxville in her work (much of which, like *The Secret Garden*, is set in England), family and scholars have noted that some of it is based on people and situations she knew during her decade as an aspiring young writer in Knoxville.

GEORGE WASHINGTON HARRIS (1814–1869), American humorist whose reckless, sometimes insensitive, and often bawdy stories are nonetheless credited with helping found an American idiom—William Faulkner and Flannery O'Connor cited him as an influence—spent most of his life in Knoxville, here he created his iconic character, Sut Lovingood.

Harris occasionally used the rough-edged frontier town as a setting.

RICHARD MARIUS (1933–1999), whose novels are mostly set in rural communities outside of the city, used more of Knoxville in his last novel, *An Affair of Honor*.

MARKET ST LOOKING TOWARDS MARKET SQUARE, EARLY 1900S

DETAIL OF THE KNOXVILLE MUSIC HISTORY MURAL ON EAST JACKSON AVE

KNOXVILLE BLUES

Today, Knoxville is host to an opera festival (America's only Rossini Festival) and an internationally acclaimed avant-garde music festival (Big Ears), both of them 21st-century developments. But Knoxville's influence on American popular music has been unpredictable and sometimes profound.

By some accounts, street music was part of the scene in Knoxville in the 1790s; little is known for certain about it, except that the city had a ballroom before it had a church.

German immigration to the area in the 1850s gave the city a leg up in terms of developing classical music, especially in the person of Gustavus Knabe, a Leipzig-born alumnus of Mendelssohn's orchestra, who organized several symphonic organizations and events in Knoxville in the post-Civil War era.

By the 1880s, the city hosted an annual Music Festival, usually emphasizing opera. However, a surprise in the 1883 festival, an old men's fiddling competition, seems to have inspired new interest in old folk music. Ever after that, country music was more and more common in town. By 1900, a few musicians were making a living in the streets, some performing their own songs.

By 1924, Knoxville-based Sterchi Brothers Furniture, in an attempt to interest working people in buying new affordable phonographs, sent local musicians to New York to make some of the first country records, among them George Reneau, Charlie Oaks, Mac and Bob, and Uncle Dave Macon.

TENNESSEE RAMBLERS

Some performers played COUNTRY FIDDLE *in the daytime and* CLASSICAL VIOLIN *at night*

BERTHA WALBURN CLARK AND HER LITTLE SYMPHONY AT THE FARRAGUT HOTEL. CA. 1915

Meanwhile, live-music radio, featuring more jazz than country, was gaining a foothold, employing multiple local musicians. In 1929 and 1930, the Brunswick/Vocalion label came to Knoxville to make a series of commercial field recordings, and found music of almost every genre, jazz, blues, gospel, and a great deal of country. Among those who recorded here were the original Tennessee Chocolate Drops, featuring Carl Martin and Howard Armstrong; gospel-blues singer Leola Manning; and the Tennessee Ramblers, featuring Willie Seivers, country's first female lead guitarist.

ROY ACUFF (LEFT) ON WNOX RADIO

The economy dampened the reception of the original releases in 1930. However, the entire experiment was internationally released as a box set called *The Knoxville Sessions* in 2016, nominated for a Grammy for its narrative.

By 1935, a brash young fiddler from Fountain City, a former athlete and bootlegger named Roy Acuff, was becoming a local phenomenon, attracting hundreds of boys and young men to his shows, some of them to witness a strange new instrument called the dobro. The unexpected development inspired the 90-minute daily variety show on WNOX called the "Mid-Day Merry-Go-Round," which helped launch the careers of numerous musicians, including bandleader Pee Wee King, singer and comedian Archie Campbell, and guitarist Chet Atkins, who lived in Knoxville in the early 1940s just for the radio opportunity. Later, Kitty Wells, Don Gibson, and others performed on the iconic show that drew crowds in the hundreds every day.

The same year that Acuff went ballistic, 1935, the Knoxville Symphony Orchestra began its first of more than 80 seasons, under the baton of Cincinnati-trained violinist Bertha Walburn Clark, to this day one of relatively few female conductors of American orchestras. The KSO was more relevant to country music than might be assumed; some fiddlers in the daytime became violinists at night.

CAS WALKER, DEMAGOGUE-IMPRESARIO

By the 1940s, Cas Walker, on WROL, was offering another option, a new form of country music called bluegrass, and his show nurtured several of the first generation of bluegrass groups. Flatt and Scruggs, mutineers from Bill Monroe's famous Blue Grass Boys, moved to Knoxville to make their first recordings and hone their radio act.

BROWNIE MCGHEE (LEFT) AND STICK MCGHEE (RIGHT) AND FRIENDS

Meanwhile, Knoxville natives Brownie and Stick McGhee, brothers with different blues styles, were coming to the fore, Brownie concentrating on country blues, playing with Woody Guthrie and his longtime partner Sonny Terry, as Stick was excited by R&B; his 1949 recording of his own song, "Drinkin' Wine, Spo-dee-o-dee," the first-ever hit for Atlantic Records, is considered one of the first rock 'n' roll disks.

By 1955, local high-schoolers the Everly Brothers, newcomers from Iowa, began experimenting with rock 'n' roll on WROL.

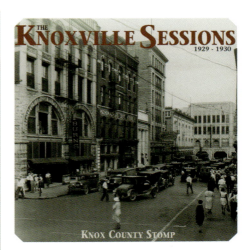

THE KNOXVILLE SESSIONS EARNED A GRAMMY NOMINATION FOR ITS LINER NOTES

Falling out of favor with their sponsor, Cas Walker, they accepted Chet Atkins' offer to work in Nashville.

Cas showed better instincts with his next discovery, a talented girl from Sevier County named Dolly Parton. The launch of her astronomical career as a singer, and songwriter, between 1958 and 1964, came at the end of the local-radio era, and of Knoxville's most famous era as a generator of fresh country music. The Mid-Day Merry-Go-Round closed shop in 1962, just as Dolly's career was taking off. However, today public-radio station WDVX pays homage to that tradition with its daily live show, the Blue Plate Special, which highlights new talent every week.

DOLLY PARTON, 1960S

Pick up a brochure and map at the

★ **VISITORS CENTER** at 301 S. Gay Street and head out around downtown on a self-directed "Cradle of Country Music" walking tour with 19 stops showcasing Knoxville's musical heritage.

DOLLY PARTON *wrote that she first* "FELL IN LOVE WITH" HER AUDIENCE *at a* WIVK *show in* 1958

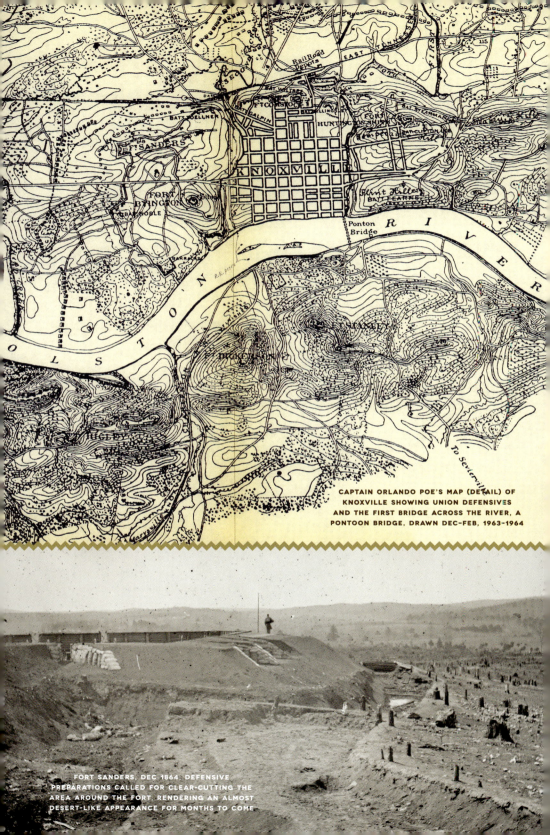

CAPTAIN ORLANDO POE'S MAP (DETAIL) OF KNOXVILLE SHOWING UNION DEFENSIVES AND THE FIRST BRIDGE ACROSS THE RIVER, A PONTOON BRIDGE, DRAWN DEC-FEB, 1963-1964

FORT SANDERS, DEC 1864; DEFENSIVE PREPARATIONS CALLED FOR CLEAR-CUTTING THE AREA AROUND THE FORT, RENDERING AN ALMOST DESERT-LIKE APPEARANCE FOR MONTHS TO COME

THE CIVIL WAR

Knoxville's battle is not one of the war's most famous, but the city's experience with the Civil War was absolute. Although only a handful of buildings remain from that time, there are still a dozen places you can go to see traces of the war and its aftermath. Knoxville's Civil War stories reflect the passions and perils of the whole country during that unsettling, sometimes horrific, and ultimately nation-changing era.

In its first 70 years, Knoxville was never dominated by any one region. Several of the city's founders were Pennsylvanians, and the early 1800s saw a peculiar influx of New Englanders. A few Deep Southerners also lived here, among them some owners of Southern plantations. By the 1850s, hundreds of Irish, Swiss, and German immigrants had arrived, many of them just learning English and the context of American politics.

Knoxville had slavery, but few businesses depended on it. Most of Knoxville's black population was enslaved, many of them working as domestic servants or assistants, in small numbers. Perhaps one in four black Knoxvillians were free, and some ran their own businesses.

Although East Tennessee had witnessed an early blooming of abolitionism in the 1820s, divisions sharpened in the 1850s, and pro-slavery sentiment became vocal and dominant. Still, even slave owners were split about whether maintaining the status quo was worth going to war.

In 1860, secession fever seemed to afflict mainly the Deep South. After the early battles, though, Tennessee, surrounded on three sides by rebel states, began to tilt toward an alliance with the Confederacy. When it did, East Tennessee Unionists proposed splitting away from Tennessee, just as West Virginia had split from Virginia. It almost happened.

Through it all, Knoxville was a mixture of Confederate partisans, Union partisans, and a number of citizens who lacked strong convictions or alliances and hoped the war would end soon.

Knoxville's most prominent Unionist was "Parson" W.G. Brownlow, a Virginia-born Methodist preacher who was best known as a newspaper editor and provocateur. Although his paper, the *Knoxville Whig*, was aimed at a local audience, his colorful abuse of secessionists earned him subscribers in the north—but he was hanged in effigy as far away as Texas.

On the other hand, Knoxville's fiercest secessionists were physician-historian J.G.M. Ramsey, whose father had moved here from Pennsylvania—and John Mitchel, the former Irish revolutionary living as an exile in America, who became attached to the secessionist cause. He probably never saw a slave before his arrival in 1854, but Mitchel extolled both slavery and secession in his Knoxville-based magazine, *The Southern Citizen*.

Violence arrived in the form of street shootings days after the firing on Ft. Sumter. Confederate recruitment sometimes took place within sight of large Union rallies. Knoxville was America's only city to be represented, simultaneously, in both U.S. Congress and Confederate Congress.

1850 Knoxville was home to 598 BLACKS, 462 ENSLAVED and 136 FREE

Remarkably, Brownlow kept publishing his pro-Union paper even after Confederate occupation, until he was arrested in December, 1861. Knoxville became essentially a military camp during the war, occupied by armies who sometimes outnumbered the citizenry.

Knoxville witnessed the military hangings of four of the famous "bridge burners," Unionist civilians who sabotaged Confederate supply lines early in the war, among them noted potter Christopher Haun.

President Lincoln was especially anxious about liberating East Tennessee, perhaps with personal motives. His father had once lived in East Tennessee, as had other family members—and the president was close to one Knoxvillain, trusted ally Horace Maynard, the rare Southerner who kept his seat in Congress after Secession.

Though it was a landlocked part of the South, Knox County's most famous native combatant was a Union Navy man, Admiral David Glasgow Farragut, whose victories at New Orleans and Mobile all but assured the Confederacy's ultimate defeat.

In June, 1863, U.S. Col. William Sanders led a federal cavalry raid on Knoxville, inflicting casualties. However, Knoxville was presumed to be so safe that it entertained Confederate

BELLE BOYD, CONFEDERATE SPY

celebrities: the vivacious young Belle Boyd—the most celebrated, if not most effective, rebel spy summered with relatives in Knoxville—and Gen. Joseph Johnston, who spent some weeks here mapping out defensive strategies.

That idyll ended with the summer, when a crisis near Chattanooga drew Confederate forces from Knoxville to help with what became the rebel victory at Chickamauga.

During their absence, U.S. Gen. Burnside, closer than Confederates realized he was, seized the opportunity to occupy Knoxville. His triumphant entrance into town was hailed with an illustration on the cover of *Harper's*. That fall, Union engineer Orlando Poe planned almost 20 forts, large and small, to encircle the city.

DETAIL OF HARPER'S COVER OCTOBER 24, 1863

In Chattanooga, Gen. Braxton Bragg regretted the loss of Knoxville and sent one of his ablest commanders to retake Knoxville from Burnside. James Longstreet questioned the Knoxville operation, but set off with 15,000 troops. Burnside and his men were ready to greet the Confederates.

① The Knoxville area's second-biggest Civil War battle, the **BATTLE OF CAMPBELL'S STATION**, occurred on Nov. 16, 1863, between Longstreet's Confederates, arriving from the west, and Burnside's Union defenders, meeting them on the east, both of them roughly along Kingston Pike. The skirmish was more costly for the Confederates, and slowed their advance toward Knoxville.

Longstreet attempted to surround the city, but was frustrated in doing so by well-established Union positions on the south side, especially at lofty, substantial Fort Dickerson. Confederates under Porter Alexander, famous artillery commander of Gettysburg, did establish a fearsome cannon battery on the bluffs downstream.

1863 | GEN. AMBROSE BURNSIDE *defended Knoxville with more than* 20,000 UNION TROOPS

"BATTLE OF CAMPBELL STATION, 1863" BY PAUL J. LONG

Longstreet might have starved Knoxville out, despite limited supplies arriving on unmanned rafts from Union supporters upriver. But Gen. Sherman was reported to be on his way, after the victory at Chattanooga—made much easier for the Union army by the absence of Longstreet and his troops encountering unexpected trouble with taking Knoxville.

At the icy dawn of Nov. 29, a desperate charge by thousands of Confederate troops on the Union army's largest fort collapsed in a near-slaughter, described as the war's bloodiest 20 minutes. During the

2 BATTLE OF FORT SANDERS, a Confederate soldier died every 11 seconds. One was wounded every two seconds.

Recognizing the disaster, Longstreet withdrew. Sherman arrived days later, and though he expressed dismay about what he considered to be exaggerated reports of Knoxville's dire circumstances, he also remarked that it was the best-fortified citadel he'd ever seen.

Knoxville remained securely in Union hands for the war's final 16 months. During that period, hundreds of the occupying soldiers were "Colored Troops," black soldiers in Union uniform. It was one of the first times in American history that blacks had some authority over whites. Predictably, there was postwar violence, which included two lynchings, one of a white former Confederate soldier hanged for murdering a former Unionist, and one a black Union soldier hanged for murdering a former Union officer.

The occupation ended in 1866, thanks to the work of Tennessee's first Republicans. Parson Brownlow, the vituperative editor, became a staunch Lincoln man and an effective—some would say extreme—supporter of civil rights for the former slaves. Even more surprisingly, he was elected governor of Tennessee. Thanks to Brownlow's strong-arm tactics, Tennessee passed the 13th and 14th amendments—even faster than some Northern states. Quickly reinstated into the Union, Tennessee never had to deal with Reconstruction's oppressions after 1866. Locally, blacks benefited from the rapid change. Knoxville became, in 1869, one of America's first cities to elect blacks to city government.

But war-related violence, including gunfights and murders, usually between whites, lasted into the 1870s.

At the brief Battle of Fort Sanders, the **CONFEDERATES LOST** 813 **MEN**; *the* **FEDERALS** *only* 13

ASSUALT ON FORT SANDERS, A LATER IMAGINATIVE ILLUSTRATION

CIVIL WAR SITES

Knoxville preserved little of its antebellum architectural heritage—very few buildings downtown are confirmed to date from the Civil War. What does remain is worth pointing out.

 ## Lamar House

Located at 803 South Gay Street
SEE BIJOU THEATRE P.50

The Lamar House—the front portion of that's now the Bijou Theatre—was Knoxville's finest hotel during the war era. In May, 1861, Confederate recruits in this building shot and killed Union demonstrator Charles Douglass on Gay Street. In early 1863, Gen. Joseph Johnston set up a temporary headquarters in this building to consider strategy. He had an unexpected but moving reunion, ironic in retrospect, with the elderly slave woman who helped raise him. About the same time, rebel spy Belle Boyd enjoyed dances here, during an interim when she was ordered to Knoxville for her own safety.

During Union occupation, it was here that mortally wounded Brig. Gen. William Sanders was carried, and here that he died—

BRIG. GEN. WILLIAM SANDERS, UNION ARMY

and where his body was concealed, because Gen. Burnside feared the impact Sanders' death would have on the morale of troops under siege. He was buried secretly downtown, but word got around, and the Knoxville garrison's newly improved major fort was named in his honor just before it became famous for fending off a major assault. A recent plaque on the front of the building commemorates Sanders' death.

And it was here—in 1871, six years after the war was supposedly over—that Alabama lawyer James Clanton, well-known former

Knoxville was a DESTINATION *for* ESCAPEES *from* CONFEDERATE PRISON CAMPS *in the Carolinas*

Confederate general, died, after he was shot by a former Union officer in a war-related dispute on Gay Street. Clanton, Ala., is named for him.

Lincoln Memorial University is named for a Civil War figure, of course, and it's appropriate that its law school operates in a building that played a major role in the war. Known as the **DEAF & DUMB ASYLUM**—a polite term, in the mid-19th century, for a School for the Deaf—was used first by the Confederates as the "Asylum Hospital." When they withdrew, they took their surgeons and orderlies and their hospital's name, opening other "Asylum Hospitals" in the Deep South, named for this building.

Meanwhile, the Union army occupied it in September, 1863, and it became a central hospital for the region for men with war-related illnesses and injuries. For more than a year, there were two Asylum Hospitals operating at the same time, one Union, one Confederate, in different states, but both named for this building.

More than a dozen downtown buildings were built in the reviving city soon after the war by Civil War veterans, some of whom

THE FORMER TENNESSEE SCHOOL FOR THE DEAF IS NOW LINCOLN MEMORIAL UNIVERSITY'S DUNCAN SCHOOL OF LAW

GEN. AMBROSE BURNSIDE, UNION ARMY

arrived unexpectedly due to the fortunes of war. Peter Kern, a wounded Confederate infantryman from Germany by way of Georgia, built the prominent Kern building at 1 Market Square. On Gay Street, the Woodruff and Tailor Lofts buildings were built by former Union officers, as was the Foundry, the last remnant of the old post-war Knoxville Iron Co., established by former Ohioan Hiram Chamberlain, once Burnside's quartermaster.

Fewer than 40 antebellum houses—perhaps one percent of all the houses that stood in Knox County in 1860—survive as preserved structures, but several of them played a role in the war. Knoxville's notoriously commercial strip, Kingston Pike, approximates the slow eastward approach of Longstreet and his army. Some antebellum homes along the pike, still visible among the commercial signage, were settings for dramatic moments in the siege. The **AVERY RUSSELL HOUSE**, *(see p.140)* a ca. 1820 tavern at 11401 Kingston Pike, was central to the Battle of Campbell Station in the early part of the siege of Knoxville. It served as a temporary hospital during that skirmish.

⑤ The **KENNEDY-BAKER HOUSE**, at 9320 Kingston Pike, and the nearby
⑥ **BAKER-PETERS HOUSE**, 9000 Kingston Pike, were homes of brothers William Baker and Harvey Baker, both of them medical doctors. The latter home, at Peters Road, was that of Dr. Harvey Baker, who was murdered by rogue Union troops during Sanders' unsuccessful raid on Knoxville in June, 1863. Bullet holes in a door in the house purportedly date from that fatal shooting. His son, Abner, was a Confederate soldier away at war, who, when he returned, killed a former Unionist in downtown Knoxville, and was promptly lynched for the deed. Baker's motive was ostensibly revenge for the doctor's murder, but no one knows for certain, considering both men died the same day. The house has been a restaurant and jazz club over the years, but it now serves as offices.

ABNER BAKER MEMORIAL STONE

KENNEDY-BAKER HOUSE

⑦ At 598 S. Peters Rd., overlooking the Pike, is **STATESVIEW**, a private residence built in 1806. During the war it was the home of Frederick Heiskell, Maryland-born journalist and politician whose career illustrates the war's complications. As his former paper, the *Knoxville Register*, tilted pro-Confederate, the elderly Heiskell was a defiant Unionist, jailed at age 75 for refusing the Confederate oath—as two of his sons who grew up in this house joined the Confederate cause. One became a Confederate

BAKER-PETERS HOUSE

The **ABNER BAKER MURDER** *has been a fertile source of* **GHOST STORIES**

KNOLLWOOD

 5 CRESCENT BEND

Located at 2728 Kingston Pike
SEE HISTORIC HOMES P.28

Crescent Bend, built in the 1834 by Drury Paine Armstrong, father of Robert Houston Armstrong, was briefly the headquarters of Confederate Gen. Joseph Kershaw, hero of Gettysburg and Chickamauga, just before the final attack on Fort Sanders. This was the closest general's headquarters to the front lines. It's now open as a museum house known for its furniture and silver collections, and its breathtaking terraced gardens leading all the way down to the river.

congressman, one a Confederate colonel. Heiskell survived the war as a conservative who, parting with the radical Unionists, supported President Johnson, accepting emancipation but not voting rights for blacks. At age 80 he ran for Congress but lost. Statesview is not open to visitors.

8 KNOLLWOOD, built for a Mexican War major atop Bearden Hill at 6411 Kingston Pike, became Gen. James Longstreet's first Knox County headquarters in the early days of the siege. It now serves as an office, and is not open to the public, but a state plaque about its war significance stands on the Pike.

 7 MABRY-HAZEN HOUSE

Located at 1711 Dandridge Avenue
SEE HISTORIC HOMES P.32

On the other side of town is the Mabry-Hazen House, built in 1858, as the home of Joseph Mabry, whose financial support for the Confederacy earned the non-soldier the honorific, "General Mabry." Confederate Gen. Felix Zollicoffer, a former newspaperman and U.S. congressman, established his headquarters here, months before he was killed in action in Kentucky. Despite Mabry's early support for the Confederacy, he was a pragmatic businessman who, after more than two years of Confederate occupation, welcomed Union officers to town in September, 1863. Mabry's Hill became an important part of the eastern defense of the city.

It's a short walk from Knoxville's Confederate Cemetery, a.k.a. Bethel Cemetery, a small fenced-off plot with limited hours.

6 BLEAK HOUSE

Located at 3148 Kingston Pike
SEE HISTORIC HOMES P.31

CANNON BALL HOLE

Bleak House, or Confederate Memorial Hall, was Longstreet's main headquarters during the Battle of Knoxville.

BLEAK HOUSE *shows more* SCARS *of* WAR *than any other historic house*

CIVIL WAR

Bethel Cemetery

Located at 1917 Bethel Avenue
SEE CEMETERIES P.167

More than 1,600 graves are unmarked; its chief feature is the lofty Confederate monument, a tall marble shaft topped with a dashing but unnamed soldier. Most of those interred here are believed to be enlisted men who died of either wounds or disease in the East Tennessee campaigns. Almost a quarter of them died in the siege of Knoxville.

BETHEL CEMETERY ALSO KNOWN AS CONFEDERATE CEMETERY

RUINS AND PARKS

Almost all of Burnside's impressive earthworks, the ring of forts engineered by Capt. Orlando Poe that so impressed Gen. Sherman in 1863, have vanished, over the years, some of them developed away soon after the troops left. (Some believe that part of Fort Sanders survives in the irregular topography of that neighborhood, between 16th and 18th Streets.)

 Some remain. The eroded rifle pits of **FORT STANLEY**, on private property on a hilltop east of Chapman Highway, require a winter without foliage and a learned guide to discern.

However, some fort sites on the rugged south side of the river have never been developed. Two of them are both preserved and open to the public.

10 Fort Dickerson

Located at 3000 Fort Dickerson Road
SEE PARKS & GARDENS P.153

Fort Dickerson was critical to the Union defense to hold these heights from which enemy cannons could seriously damage the city. Though never assaulted, Fort Dickerson traded artillery fire with an advance guard of Confederates early in the siege of Knoxville. Supplied with a road, it has been a public park since 1957. It drew thousands in 1963 when it was the site of a noisy centennial re-enactment.

FORT DICKERSON

 FORT **H**IGLEY / **H**IGH **G**ROUND **P**ARK

Located at 1000 Cherokee Trail
SEE PARKS & GARDENS P.153

Nearby, as the crow flies—but several miles by road, and more easily accessible from Alcoa Highway—is a much-smaller Union position, Fort Higley. For decades, the earthworks were known only to the most intrepid Civil War buffs willing to thrash through the underbrush, and perhaps trespass, to behold it. It became better known to the public at large in the early 21st century when it was threatened with a major condo development project.

The charitable Aslan Foundation purchased the property and established High Ground Park on Cherokee Trail, completed just in time for the sesquicentennial of the siege of Knoxville in 2013. Now with parking and easy paths, it offers abundant signage about the more furtive battles on the south side of the river. The "redan," or small fortified cannon emplacement, is no bigger than a boxing ring, but a rarity. Long sought by daring hikers, it's now easier and safe.

FORT HIGLEY AT HIGH GROUND PARK

Although there's no confirming record of it, archaeologists believe an odd earthen bulwark west of town along the Third Creek Greenway, near the parking lot off Sutherland Avenue, is a Civil War remnant, there to protect the railroad trestle over the creek. Railroad trestles were often targets of sabotage, especially in East Tennessee. Signage explains the theory. (Although the picturesque masonry trestle there today looks historic, it's post-Civil War.)

Each UNION FORT *was* NAMED *for an* OFFICER *who died in East Tennessee campaigns*

National Cemetery

Located at 939 Tyson St
SEE CEMETERIES P.164

A vivid legacy of the war is the National Cemetery, one of the first national cemeteries established in America, and a rarity for its concentric-circle "wagon wheel" design. Gen. Burnside established this 10-acre plot as a soldiers' burying ground days after his arrival in Knoxville in 1863. It would eventually receive about 3,500 burials of Union soldiers who died in regional campaigns, including several who died in the defense of Fort Sanders, but many who died as far away as Kentucky or North Carolina. Among them are scores of "colored troops," black soldiers involved in the Union occupation of formerly Confederate cities like Knoxville. A third of the Civil War-era graves are marked "Unknown."

UNION SOLDIERS MONUMENT AT KNOXVILLE'S NATIONAL CEMETERY

Most of those buried here are enlisted men, but Union Gen. Joseph Cooper, combat veteran of several battles who commanded a brigade in the successful Franklin and Nashville campaigns, and survived the war, is an exception. Nearby Cooper Street is named for him.

The Union monument, one of the South's largest, was originally installed in 1901, with many veterans present. However, in 1904, a lightning bolt hit the bronze eagle on top, destroying it. It was replaced with a marble non-conductive Union soldier in 1906. The National Cemetery's burials reflect veterans of every American war since, but to this day, more than a third of its graves memorialize the dead of the Civil War.

While you're there, you might also consider a stroll through Old Gray.

 ## Old Gray

Located at 543 North Broadway
865-522-1424 • oldgraycemetery.org
SEE CEMETERIES P.163

Established in 1850 and named for Thomas Gray, the English poet (not the Confederacy), Old Gray is the final resting place of numerous major figures on both sides of the war, including journalist-governor "Parson" W.G. Brownlow; Congressman Horace Maynard; journalist and Union Capt. William Rule; Confederate militia Gen. William Caswell who died in 1862, not in battle but as a victim of an unsolved murder; and Confederate Col. Henry Ashby, who was shot to death in the streets by U.S. Maj. Eldad Cicero Camp, who is also buried here. The Horne family plot contains a small statue of a Confederate soldier, in memory of two enlisted men in that plot.

HORACE MAYNARD MEMORIAL AT OLD GRAY CEMETERY

The war's most violent moment locally was the assault on Fort Sanders, which is commemorated only by two quiet monuments. On 17th Street, between Clinch and Laurel, is a small marble marker, installed in 1914 when there were still ruins of Fort Sanders nearby (they were gone by the 1920s), commemorating the death of 129 Confederate soldiers near that spot.

At the corner of Clinch and 16th is a larger, castle-like Union monument. It honors the New York Highlanders, the regiment defending Fort Sanders from the Confederate attack. Installed in 1918, during World War I, it emphasized reconciliation with an unusual relief of Union and Confederate soldiers shaking hands.

CONFEDERATE MONUMENT AT 17TH ST BETWEEN CLINCH AVE AND LAUREL AVE

MUSEUMS & EXHIBITS

Combining maps, a film, and artifacts presented in the context of where they were found, UT's McClung Museum features a permanent exhibit about the war in Knoxville, and gives the best overview of the war here *(see p.40)*.

A substantial part of the Museum of East Tennessee History covers the Civil War and its complexities. Among its rarest artifacts is the desk Horace Maynard used in U.S. Congress when he was stubbornly representing his district in a state that considered itself part of the Confederacy *(see p.37)*.

The Farragut Museum displays an impressive array of the personal effects of the U.S. Navy's first admiral, including his shipboard desk, as well as a collection of rare scrimshaw carvings on whale teeth depicting Civil War naval battles *(see p.42)*.

UNION MONUMENT AT 16TH ST AND CLINCH AVE

Fort Sanders' ruins are mentioned in James Agee's A DEATH IN THE FAMILY, *set in 1916*

THE HILL, CA. 1879, ABOUT THE TIME EAST TENNESSEE UNIVERSITY BECAME THE UNIVERSITY OF TENNESSEE

UNIVERSITY OF TENNESSEE

The University of Tennessee can't be mistaken for any other college campus.

UT thoroughly occupies one broad peninsula of the Tennessee River. Included in that peninsula are two sizeable creeks and one extraordinarily steep hill, which for a century served as the entirety of campus. "The Hill" remains a distinctive icon, and has its own history, almost two centuries of academia. Tens of thousands of professors have lectured to more than half a million students here.

But much of the campus's story is about the remaining traces of older, nonacademic uses of what would have been a dramatic neighborhood even with no proximity to a university. It may be the world's only college campus that includes both an authentic prehistoric Indian mound as well as sites associated with both Confederate and Union positions during a desperate Civil War battle.

The founding date "1794," visible all over campus, would make UT one of the oldest public universities in America—though that date conceals a complicated story. That was the year a Presbyterian minister named Samuel Carrick and a few supporters, some of them Revolutionary War veterans and a couple of them future governors or senators, started a tiny school of higher learning in a single frame house in downtown Knoxville, before the state of Tennessee even existed. It was called Blount College, after the territorial governor, who also happened to be on the Board of Trustees. After Carrick's premature death in 1809, it closed for 11 years. What had become known as East Tennessee College revived and moved to its present campus, the hilltop on the west side of town in 1828. There it became East Tennessee University. It was not fully fledged as the statewide University of Tennessee until 1879.

All those dates make it pretty old, and its campus tells an interesting story.

The Hill

Entrance off Cumberland Avenue at Circle Drive

UT's 1928 alma mater begins, "On a hallowed hill in Tennessee, like a beacon shining bright / The stately walls of old UT rise glorious to the sight...."

The Hill is still as steep as it ever was, a daunting eminence, a Tennessee Acropolis. Hill-climbing is part of the UT experience. On its eastern side, Second Creek, seen as a natural amenity for a college in the 1820s, separates the campus from downtown. It's still there to see. From the peaceful creek, you'll climb 235 steps to the Hill's summit.

For a century, the Hill constituted the university's whole campus. Now a small part of UT's acreage, it still holds a symbolic place of honor.

In 1826, when workers began digging a foundation for the hilltop's first building, they encountered a grisly surprise. Human bones were all that was left of a military cemetery of the 1790s. The frontier community had turned over so fast that a once-prominent graveyard was forgotten in just 30 years.

UT was **OUTSIDE** *of* **KNOXVILLE'S CITY LIMITS** *until* 1897

AYRES HALL ON THE HILL

That new building, eventually known as Old College, included a lofty bell tower. A populist politician denounced it as "this melancholy building, raising its proud front on an isolated hill, until you become exhausted to reach the summit."

The Civil War divided the university's leadership, and the college closed for the duration. In 1863, Union positions on the Hill became known as Fort Byington, a federal battery helping to protect Union-held Knoxville from the expected Confederate siege. It drew fire from Confederate cannons, leaving scars on the college buildings that remained evident into the 20th century.

Meanwhile, Confederates were firing cannons from positions on the far western edge of campus, what's now Sorority Village. Archaeological digs in 2009 turned up multiple rebel artifacts there.

Trenchwork remained for years, until UT President Thomas Humes, former Unionist and later Civil War historian, enlisted shovel-wielding students to remove war's traces from the Hill.

Reconstruction-era politics resulted in East Tennessee University achieving coveted Morrill Act status—the first Southern college to get that access to federal resources. That advantage, granted to the most Republican (pro-Union) part of the state, was a factor in ETU being designated the University of Tennessee in 1879, an honor that might otherwise have gone to a more centrally located college.

Ayres Hall

Located at 1403 Circle Drive
MON-FRI: 8AM-5PM
SUMMER HOURS VARY

Despite earnest attempts to save familiar, war-scarred Old College in 1919, it was demolished for a new building. Replacing it, more grandly, was Ayres Hall, today UT's best-known architectural symbol. Completed in 1921, it was commenced during the administration of President Brown Ayres, physics and engineering scholar from Memphis. Ayres' unexpected death in early 1919, when the project was already underway, prompted the name. Its designer was Chicago architect Grant Miller (1870–1956), a frequent consultant on UT projects for 20 years.

UT accommodates about 29,000 **STUDENTS**, *on a* 910-ACRE CAMPUS

Perhaps his most famous work, Ayres Hall is sometimes labeled "Collegiate Gothic." It is, after all, a rare local building that features actual gargoyles. However, architects insist its symmetry makes its idiosyncratic style more akin to Elizabethan Revival.

Ayres Hall's Ivy-League looks earned it a moment of Hollywood fame. In one brief scene in Ingrid Bergman's *A Walk in the Spring Rain*, shot in 1969, it represents an unnamed northeastern university.

SOUTH COLLEGE ON THE HILL

UT has no architectural remnant of its first 75 years. In fact, only one original building on campus dates to before the 20th century.

 That building, UT's oldest, is **SOUTH COLLEGE**, an 1871 red-brick building on the eastern side of the quad. It's a rare Knoxville building with anchor plates, or "earthquake bolts," more familiar in other old Southern cities. Its basement houses a snack shop that runs independently of the university by a longstanding agreement.

Austin Peay was central to a memorable incident in early 1970, prompted by anxiety about a new UT president, but perhaps reflecting the antiauthoritarian mood of the era. Hundreds of demonstrators surrounded the building, trapping administrators inside, as student leader Peter Kami challenged new president Ed Boling to "hand to hand combat." Knoxville called out riot police in gas masks, who dispersed the crowd and arrested several who became known as the "Knoxville 22." Facing federal charges, Kami later fled the country, and his fate is unknown.

4 *Austin Peay*

Located at 1404 Circle Drive
MON–FRI: 8AM–5PM
SUMMER HOURS VARY

One of the Hill's most striking buildings, west of Ayres, is Austin Peay, named for an education-minded governor. Completed as a library in 1911 but radically remodeled in the 1930s, it became the university's administration building, including the president's office and the room where the Board of Trustees met. A plaque about UT's desegregation stands there in front of the building where the decisions were made to admit black students, by degrees, from 1952 to 1961.

ORNATE ENTRANCE TO AUSTIN PEAY

GOV. AUSTIN PEAY (1875-1927) *is also* **HONOREE** *of a state university in Clarksville*

5 ALUMNI MEMORIAL HALL

Located at 1408 Middle Drive
MON-FRI: 8AM-5PM
SUMMER HOURS VARY

On the Hill's southwestern slope is Alumni Memorial Hall, completed in 1934. Intended as a memorial to UT's losses in World War I, it's one of the most distinctive designs of local architect Charles Barber, a romantic who evoked medieval styles. Its elaborate facade includes ironwork by famous metal sculptor and Ukrainian immigrant Samuel Yellin. It was intended mainly as a gymnasium complex, with basketball courts and swimming pools, and served that purpose for students and basketball fans.

Instantly, though, it became a performing-arts center, and represented a watershed in how Knoxville interacted with the university. Before 1934, Townies rarely set foot on the Hill. All entertainment was downtown. However, as the city procrastinated on building a civic auditorium, Alumni Hall drew bookings for the major shows aimed at the general public. Within a few seasons, the building had an impressive record of hosting major classical and jazz performers, from Chick Webb to Tommy Dorsey and his young singer, Frank Sinatra. Authors like Carl Sandburg and Tennessee Williams spoke here. Later, performers ranging from Nina Simone to the Clash played here. Sergei Rachmaninoff performed here in early 1943; seriously ill with cancer, the Russian composer and pianist canceled the rest of his American tour, and died weeks later. It turned out to be his final show, a distinction honored with a bronze statue on World's Fair Park *(see p.143)*.

Men's basketball moved into a new facility in 1958. Because women's sports weren't prioritized there, Coach Pat Head Summitt, who would become the winningest college basketball coach in history, scored her first victories in this building in 1975.

HOSKINS LIBRARY ON CUMBERLAND AVE

ALUMNI MEMORIAL HALL

6 HOSKINS LIBRARY

Located at 1401 Cumberland Avenue
865-974-6214 • lib.utk.edu
MON-FRI: 8AM-4PM

Hoskins Library, at the foot of the Hill across Cumberland, is another Charles Barber fantasy, with castellated parapets and a spiral staircase that could make a setting for a Hollywood swordfight. Completed in 1931, its grander original design curtailed by the Depression, it was once UT's main library, and

Alumni Memorial now houses **COX AUDITORIUM**, *better for* **CONCERTS** *than a gymnasium*

housed the office of John C. Hodges (1892–1967), the UT English scholar famous for the *Hodges Harbrace Handbook of English* both dreaded and appreciated by freshmen around the country. Much of its interior was painted by Hugh Tyler, the artistic uncle mentioned in some of James Agee's work. Its tower housed the Audigier Art Collection of European, Asian and African antiquities from 1932 until a major burglary in 1973—still unsolved today—after which the substantial remainder went to McClung Museum. The library is now the headquarters for several ongoing scholarly projects, like the Center for War and Society and the Andrew Jackson Papers.

HOSKINS LIBRARY ENTRANCE GARGOYLE

UT'S ICONIC VOLUNTEER STATUE AT CIRCLE PARK

 # CIRCLE PARK

Located at Circle Park Drive
MON–FRI: DAWN–DUSK
SEE PARKS & GARDENS P.154

Parts of UT welcome the non-scholarly public, and for a short visit, Circle Park is a good place to start.

 The iconic **VOLUNTEER STATUE** stands at the entrance to Circle Park, holding his torch toward Volunteer Boulevard. Its basic design came as the result of a nationwide competition in 1931. After some delays and alterations, it was finally installed here in 1968, soon after the completion of Volunteer Boulevard. Its flame has burned almost continuously since.

Circle Park itself seems collegiate, like a circular quad. Over the years, the shady green patch has occasionally hosted concerts, demonstrations, and speakers. However, the park was here for 70 years before it was connected to a university. Established by the 1880s in what was then a suburban area, Circle Park, first known simply as "the Circle," was arguably Knoxville's first public park. Streetcars brought people here from downtown for picnics and pick-up sports. A prestigious address, Circle Park was originally ringed with Victorian homes.

The Circle's first academic-related building was McClung Museum, completed in 1961. Designed by Barber McMurry and UT architect Malcolm Rice, McClung is a compact but far-reaching scholarly museum (*see p.40*).

EARLY 1900S POSTCARD SHOWS HOW CIRCLE PARK ONCE LOOKED

WUOT (1949) *is Knoxville's oldest continually broadcast radio station*

Nearby, the Student Services Building and the Communications Building share the same ca. 1969 modernist concrete arc. Behind is Andy Holt Tower, finished in 1973. Designed during a period of student unrest, the administrative tower assured interior egress with a controllable bridge, discouraging unruly sieges.

The Communications Building along the eastern side of Circle Park has been home to the UT *Daily Beacon* and two different public stations: stately WUOT, known for classical, jazz, and NPR, was founded in 1949; WUTK, a partly student-run station known for alternative rock, was founded in 1981. The Circle Park level features the interactive Tennessee Newspaper Hall of Fame.

 ## *Neyland Stadium*

Located at 1600 Phillip Fulmer Way
865-974-1205 • *utevents@utk.edu*
TOURS BY APPOINTMENT *Admission fee Schedule 5 days in advance*

One of America's largest athletic stadiums, Neyland Stadium was not built all at once. Peer through the superstructure and you'll see the old ca. 1948 masonry "horseshoe"

stadium. Shields-Watkins Field first appeared here in 1921, and was used for football games, track meets, and baseball games. During those first years, it offered only bleachers. It grew through more than a dozen expansions over the years. Volmania set in after 1926, when Coach Robert Neyland began leading the Vols into national contention, accelerating the stadium's growth. By 2000, it was the largest football stadium in America, with a capacity of almost 110,000. (At this writing it's still in the top five.)

GENERAL ROBERT NEYLAND STATUE AT THE STADIUM

It got its name in 1962, weeks before the famous coach's death. In May, 1970, it hosted a Billy Graham Crusade, a multi-night evangelical event that drew President Nixon during the time of the Cambodia bombings and the Kent State shootings. Vocal demonstrations during Nixon's speech resulted in dozens of arrests and national news coverage.

Neyland has enjoyed a few moments of Hollywood fame. UT anthropologist William Bass's experiments in observing how corpses decay began within his labs in the interior part to the stadium—a fact referenced in the 2009

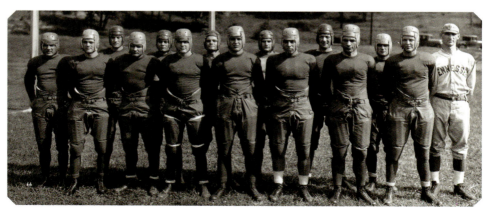

UT FOOTBALL PLAYERS, 1920S

UT's pre-1921 FIELD *included* EXPOSED ROCK *and a slight* UPHILL SLOPE

SHIELDS-WATKIN FIELD, CA. 1940

UNIVERSITY OF TENNESSEE

Best Picture nominee, *The Blind Side*. The stadium itself serves as a poignant setting for the 2018 film *The Last Movie Star*, in which Burt Reynolds plays an aging former Vol.

14 The big statue of **GEN. ROBERT NEYLAND**, installed in 2010, honors the memory of UT's most famous coach. A West Pointer and veteran of both world wars, during his time at UT (1926–52) Neyland brought military discipline to football, an offbeat defense-dominant approach that nonetheless led to several undefeated seasons and an astonishing overall record that supported several claims for national championships.

Other than the Graham Crusade, UT has only rarely allowed the stadium to be used for events other than football (and, once a year, the finale of the Knoxville Marathon). For three nights in August, 1984, the Jacksons, featuring Michael Jackson and his brothers, performed at Neyland.

Neyland's location by the river gives it a rare distinction enjoyed since the early days. At each home game, the long docks near the stadium welcome the Vol Navy, made up of as many as 200 pleasure boats convening here for a game-day weekend. (The term "sailgating" may have originated in a *Playboy* magazine feature about UT in 2006.)

PAT SUMMITT MEMORIAL AT LAKE LOUDOUN BLVD

9 **THOMPSON BOLING ARENA**, completed in 1987, is known less for its metal-clad utilitarian design than for what it has hosted. It's the building most associated **15** with the triumphs of Lady Vols Coach **PAT SUMMITT**, who coached several national-championship teams here until her retirement in 2012—her 2013 statue stands nearby—and for an impressive array of major concerts, from the likes of REM, Prince, and Stevie Wonder, as well as other major events, like the region's first visits from Cirque du Soleil.

PEYTON MANNING, *Vol quarterback 1994-1997, often* VISITS *as a* FAN

THE FREQUENTLY REPAINTED ROCK OFFERS DAILY MANIFESTOS IN FRONT OF THE NATALIE HASLAM MUSIC CENTER ON VOLUNTEER BLVD

The Natalie Haslam Music Center, the Art and Architecture Building, the Carousel, the Clarence Brown Theatre, McClung Plaza, and the Hodges Library form a modernist cultural cluster in the center of campus. Here, as nowhere else in the region, you can hear a music recital, watch a professional-quality play, see an edgy art show, attend a provocative lecture, and do some serious library research—all without even crossing a street.

10 The **ART + ARCHITECTURE BUILDING** (architects prefer the plus), designed by McCarty Holsaple McCarty was condemned as "ugly" when it was built in 1981, for its exterior's aptly named "brutalist" style, but it has since earned national praise. Even detractors find it a fun place to walk into, an interior hive of visible activity on multiple levels. Visit the Ewing Gallery, whose ever-changing and unpredictable displays of contemporary art are open to the public most days. It's named for maverick modernist C. Kermit "Buck" Ewing, who started UT's art program in 1948. (The building's creative departments also runs the UT Downtown Gallery at 106 S. Gay Street, as well as the Fab Lab, an architectural studio, at 525 N. Gay.)

11 The **NATALIE HASLAM MUSIC CENTER** is an achievement of sunlit modernism, a joint venture by local firms Barber McMurry and Blankenship and Partners, completed in 2013, replacing an earlier, plainer building on the same site. Fondly known as "The Natalie," for its beloved philanthropist, it hosts classical study, but is also home to UT's famous jazz program, which has attracted world-renowned musicians like pianist Donald Brown and saxophonist Greg Tardy. During the school year, especially in the spring, the "Natalie's" auditoriums host recitals, lectures, and visiting performers, most of them in the 400-seat, scientifically acoustic Powell Music Hall. (UT's operas are performed at the historic Bijou downtown.)

On the Natalie's front lawn, by the way, is a chunk of limestone known as "the Rock." In the 1960s, the 98-ton boulder became a natural-looking landscaping feature of Fraternity Row. In the early years it was hardly noticed, only occasionally tagged with graffiti.

ART + ARCHITECTURE BUILDING

However, by the 1990s, its ever larger and splashier repainted mottos and manifestos sometimes made the news. A redesign of this part of campus in 2009 saw the Rock moved diagonally down the street from its original location, to a position of honor as a forum for free speech.

Built in 1951 as a community project in the middle of what was then a residential 12 neighborhood, the **CAROUSEL THEATRE** is believed to be America's oldest theater-in-the-round. Unimpressive from the outside—to be fair, it was intended to be an open-air theater without walls—the

Originally a community theater, the CAROUSEL *once stood on now-vanished* SOUTH SEVENTEENTH STREET

Carousel shines in the inside, where you'll see its innovatively versatile design. Future Tony winner John Cullum began his performing career here in the 1950s, as did Collin Wilcox, memorable for her role in *To Kill a Mockingbird*. In 1976, playwright Edward Albee led a workshop here, and in the 1980s, author Alex Haley lectured here. Its modern honoree is philanthropist Ula Love Doughty, a UT alumna noted for some comic roles in Hollywood movies of the 1930s.

Clarence Brown Theatre

Located at 1714 Andy Holt Avenue 865-974-5161 • clarencebrowntheatre.com • **BOX OFFICE MON–FRI: NOON–5PM** *or 2 hrs before a show*

Clarence Brown Theatre honors its alumnus-donor, MGM director Clarence Brown, a genius who studied engineering at UT, class of 1910, before going on to a prolific career as a technically innovative director in Hollywood, especially for MGM, where he directed several of Greta Garbo's best-known movies. He was also associated with the early careers of Joan Crawford, Clark Gable, and Elizabeth Taylor, who starred in his movie *National Velvet*. Other movies helmed by Brown include *Ah, Wilderness*, *The Human Comedy*, and *Intruder in the Dust*. Brown himself endowed this award-winning theater project, designed by Knoxville's Bruce McCarty, and enabled by Brown's donation. The elderly Brown attended several shows here. Since its opening in 1970, actors like David Keith (*An Officer and a Gentleman*) and Dale Dickey (*Winters Bone*, *Leave No Trace*) began their careers here, and a few shows that started here made it to Broadway (notably the musical hit *Sugar Babies*, 1979).

ORIGINAL POSTER FROM *ANNA CHRISTIE*, DIRECTED BY CLARENCE BROWN

Oscar-nominated British actor Sir Anthony Quayle appeared on stage frequently during a three-year residency here, and speakers on this stage have included playwright Tennessee Williams (whose father was a UT alum) and author Christopher Isherwood.

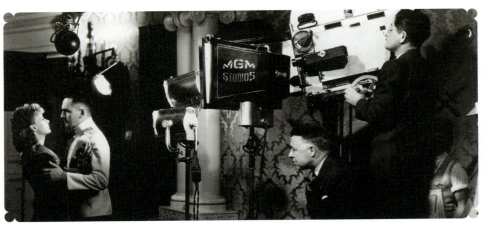

A RARE PRODUCTION SHOT FROM THE SET OF *ANNA KARENINA*, STARRING GRETA GARBO AND FREDERIC MARCH, 1935. BROWN LOOKS ON AT BOTTOM

1900 | CLARENCE BROWN *was well known in Knoxville as a* **PERFORMING ELOCUTIONIST**

THE "EUROPA AND THE BULL" STATUE BY CARL MILLES WITH THE ZIGGURAT-SHAPED HODGES LIBRARY IN THE BACKGROUND

The Clarence Brown's professional troupe, supplemented with theater students, produce multiple performances here each year, from extravagant musicals to quieter, experimental works. An intimate Lab Theater is accessed from the northern side of the building.

Completed in 1967 and a site of many dramatic events over the years from antiwar demonstrations to streaking spectacles, **14** **MCCLUNG PLAZA**, part of the McClung Tower complex, was made possible by philanthropist Ellen McClung Berry (1894–1992), whose tragically dramatic life is the subject of a recent novel; its most **13** public feature is the statue, **EUROPA AND THE BULL**, a 1924 bronze by Swedish sculptor Carl Milles.

5 Originally built in 1969, **HODGES LIBRARY**—named for the noted grammarian (*see p.105*) underwent a radical expansion and redesign in 1987, and since then has been known since as the Ziggurat. Hodges is known for its special collections of documents, images, and recordings (*see p.41*). Its many specialties include the Great Smoky Mountains Regional Project and the Modern Political Archives, including the papers of major statesmen like Howard Baker and Estes Kefauver. Multiple other collections include papers of director Clarence Brown and author James Agee. A lecture hall draws authors, poets laureate, and occasional rock stars. It includes all you'd expect in a major university's library, plus a few surprises. Its common areas often include exhibits, including a UT Alumni Academic Hall of Fame, and a long-term exhibit called "The Centaur Excavations at Volos," ostensibly the result of an archaeological dig (have a look at it and see what you think!).

At the top of the Cumberland Avenue "Strip," at the corner of Melrose, is the **15** rotunda-style **BAKER CENTER FOR PUBLIC POLICY**, a venue for lectures and exhibits about political issues and international relations named for UT alum Howard Baker (1925–2014), the former U.S. Senate majority leader known as "the Great Conciliator." Baker attended its 2008 opening and kept an office there in his later years.

SEN. HOWARD BAKER *graduated from* UT LAW SCHOOL *in* 1949

THE OLD NEIGHBORHOOD

Several buildings on the western part of campus recall a pre-campus era—as some names tell bits of the story of previous generations. Melrose Avenue and Melrose Place carry the name of an 1850s mansion, home of banker Thomas O'Conner until his death in the legendary Mabry-O'Conner shootout of 1882. After his widow's death, "Melrose" was employed for several years as an art museum before it was demolished in the 1950s for dormitory construction. Lake Avenue, at the foot of the hill, is named for the O'Conners' artificial lake, a setting for stylish Victorian-era soirées, but also long gone.

 ### Tyson Alumni House

Located at 1609 Melrose Avenue
MON-FRI: 8AM-5PM

The Tyson House, a Victorian built in the 1890s but radically remodeled in a neoclassical style, with Corinthian columns, ca. 1910, was the longtime home of a dynamic Knoxville family. Col. Lawrence Davis Tyson was a career soldier who once chased Geronimo's Apaches across the West, but who worked in Knoxville between wars as a textile industrialist and as a military instructor at UT. His wife, Bettie, was known for her parties in her terraced garden here.

LAWRENCE DAVIS TYSON EARLY IN HIS MILITARY CAREER

Tyson led troops in the Spanish-American War, and served as occupation governor of Puerto Rico. A brigadier-general during World War I, he commanded a regiment that breached the Hindenburg Line in France. Meanwhile, his son McGhee, known here as a golfer, enlisted to be a pilot in the Navy Signal Corps. In the final weeks of the war, his plane went down in the North Sea. After his body was recovered, Bettie Tyson wanted to memorialize her son by proposing that in exchange for their donation of a city park along Third Creek, Knoxville's airport always be named for McGhee Tyson.

THE TYSON HOUSE ON MELROSE AVE NAMED AFTER BRIG. GEN. LAWRENCE DAVIS TYSON, A VETERAN OF THE SPANISH-AMERICAN WAR AND WORLD WAR I

Gen. Tyson was later elected U.S. senator, and died in office in 1929. Bettie died here at home in 1933.

(*Note:* though locals have referred to this historic home as "the Tyson House" for more than a century, an Episcopal campus-ministry around the corner at 824 Melrose Place has long used the same phrase.)

MCGHEE TYSON *was a nephew of library honoree* **LAWSON MCGHEE**, *who also died young*

ℋOPECOTE

Located at 1820 Melrose Avenue

Melrose Avenue offers another glimpse of the residential neighborhood, homes of the modestly affluent. Fortunately, the most interesting house on Melrose is also perhaps the best preserved. Resembling a traditional English Cottage, Hopecote was built in 1924, employing elements of Knoxville history, including timbers from a barn on the old Farragut property. Its designer was John Fanz Staub, a Knoxville-born architect most famous for his Houston mansions. After it won a national *House Beautiful* magazine award, Hopecote inspired imitations across the country. Albert Hope, a downtown jeweler, and his wife, Emma, lived here and frequently entertained garden clubs and other gatherings. Emma Hope lived here until her death in 1977, and willed her house to the university. Today, UT employs Hopecote as a guest house.

THE AG CAMPUS

The Agricultural Campus, separated from the rest of campus by Third Creek, is famous for its veterinary school and hospital. **MORGAN HALL** (2621 Morgan Circle Dr.), was designed by Grant Miller in 1919 as a companion piece to Ayres Hall— though it's more than half a mile away. It's named for Prof. Harcourt Morgan (1867–1950). The Canadian-born entomologist became president of UT as it was being built. In 1933, Morgan was selected by Franklin Roosevelt to be one of the original three directors of the Tennessee Valley Authority. Known in the 1980s as the "trial garden," **UT GARDENS** formerly resembled an outdoor laboratory. In fact it still is that. But UT Gardens, near the mouth of Third Creek, have since been groomed for public enjoyment, with some whimsical aspects especially for kids. It even hosts weddings. (By the way, the Gardens are near the northern anchor of the unique cross-river cable car that ferried passengers up cables to a prospective park at the top of the bluffs until a fatal accident in 1894 ended the attraction.)

The **WAR DOG MEMORIAL** at the Neyland Drive entrance is a Knoxville curiosity. Dedicated in 1998 as a memorial to loyal canines who have served the U.S. military, the statue of an alert Doberman is a copy of a monument at the War Dog Cemetery in Guam. There are other war-dog memorials in America, but this may be the only one not associated with a military facility.

WAR DOG MEMORIAL AT THE VET SCHOOL

The oldest structure in Knoxville is perhaps the campus's most extraordinary distinction. It dates to the 7th Century A.D. UT'S **INDIAN MOUND** is a small but sharply pronounced hill alongside Joe Johnson Drive, the better preserved of two marked Indian mounds in Knoxville. Its builders were the Woodland Indians, for lack of knowledge of whatever these Native Americans called themselves, and is believed to be a burial mound.

PREHISTORIC INDIAN MOUND ON JOE JOHNSON DR

The INDIAN MOUND *was a* VICTORIAN-ERA TOURIST ATTRACTION

UT GARDENS ON NEYLAND DR

MORGAN HALL, NAMED AFTER PROFESSOR HARCOURT MORGAN, UT PRESIDENT

UNIVERSITY OF TENNESSEE

FOURTH & GILL NEIGHBORHOOD

NEIGHBORHOODS

NORTH

North Knoxville was once known for grand residences, comfortable neighborhoods, and important factories. Its main street is Broadway, a 19th-century road originally known as Broad Street. It connects downtown's Henley Street to Maynardville, and on the way bisects historic North Knoxville and skirts Sharp's Ridge to serve the heart of Fountain City. Once an avenue of mansions (it still boasts 1890's Greystone) and small factories, Broadway still has its charms, roughly tracing the route of First Creek, central Knoxville's main tributary.

In the late 19th century, as Knoxville suburbanized, hundreds who had grown up in close quarters downtown wanted to live the new, modern American lifestyle in freestanding single-family homes with small lots, grassy lawns, and picket fences. Old North and Fourth and Gill were once considered part of North Knoxville, a separately incorporated suburb whose first mayor was German immigrant Louis Gratz. Many of the early residents of North Knoxville were first and second generation German and Irish families.

In the 20th century, development patterns made portions of North Knoxville seem like different neighborhoods. The wedge west of Broadway and east of Central has been known since the 1970s as Old North. The area east of Broadway and west of Hall of Fame Drive (or I-40, in the only spot in town where it takes a north-south jag) is Fourth and Gill, named for a notable intersection.

Fourth & Gill

Fourth and Gill is a classic Victorian neighborhood, with few mansions but lots of comfortable middle-class homes, built close to each other and mostly renovated, but with considerable individuality. Fourth and Gill's most famous resident was probably Robert Taylor (1850–1912), not just a popular governor and U.S. senator, but also an early proponent of country music (he was a fiddler himself), and a funny and charismatic speaker.

Taylor lived right at the corner of Fourth and Gill, in the neighborhood's largest house, known as "the Governor's Mansion," notable for its porches and cone-topped tower so tall it peaked above the elevated interstate. It was burned down in 1985 by an arsonist who confessed he burned it down because he thought it was "ugly." Its plot, vacant for years, eventually became a park.

Attractions in Fourth and Gill include a couple of lovely old churches, like the impressive Gothic Revival monument in brick and stone known as Central United Methodist (1927) on Third Avenue—and the house at 820 North Fourth, not because it's one of the neighborhood's more eye-catching

In the early 20th century, CIRCUSES *set up on the* NORTH CENTRAL FAIRGROUNDS

Victorians, but because it has housed Sassy Ann's, an unusual multi-level nightclub that has been operating under several different names since the 1970s. Nearby, at the intersection of Fourth and Gill, is the Birdhouse, at 800 N. Fourth, a multi-function community gathering and art space that has hosted art shows, poetry readings, and radio broadcasts.

Near Fourth and Gill is a rare remnant of an era when Broadway was lined with gilded-age mansions. At 1306 N. Broadway, Greystone (1890), built for Union veteran and millionaire investor Eldad Cicero Camp, is the last-known work of well-known Washington architect Alfred Mullett. Since 1961 it has been the headquarters of local TV station WATE.

GREYSTONE, HOME TO WATE TV 6

OLD NORTH, to the north and west of Fourth and Gill between Broadway and North Central, has some Victorian homes, too, but perhaps more early 20th century houses, including some in the Craftsman tradition. Many of its original residents were associated with one of Knoxville's biggest industries, Brookside Mills, a fabric factory that specialized in woven products. The factory opened just to the west of the neighborhood in 1885 and employed thousands before it closed in 1956. Both factory workers and management lived in the neighborhood, the latter in larger houses along the ridgetops.

CENTRAL UNITED METHODIST CHURCH

Happy Holler

Alongside Old North is a historic mini-downtown along North Central at Anderson, a distinct pocket of fun fondly known since about 1900 as Happy Holler. It started about 1885 when an Irish immigrant named Kavanaugh noticed that many farmers' wagons seemed to have trouble negotiating a steep dip in the road into Knoxville. As wagons got stuck in the mud, or broke axels, he figured they could use a drink, and opened a saloon here. It was a hit, aided by the fact that the nearby Brookside Mill was opening about the same time. For years, despite the presence of the gorgeous Holy Ghost Catholic Church, Happy Holler had a rough reputation, with multiple beer joints and a boxing ring (world heavyweight champ Big

HAPPY HOLLER *is just part of the reviving area now known as* DOWNTOWN NORTH

LOOKING SOUTH ON BROADWAY AT CENTRAL WITH THE "FLAT IRON" BUILDING IN CENTER, WITH ST. JOHN'S LUTHERAN CHURCH IN THE BACKGROUND (RIGHT), 1920S

John Tate trained here in the '70s). It's much revived today, with restaurants and bars, a big food co-op, an unusual performance venue, a rare-record store, a walk-up ice-cream and hot-dog stand, the almost indescribable Time Warp Tea Room, and a rejuvenated ca. 1930 movie theater, the Central Cinema.

North Central has been in a state of rapid renovation in recent years, with bakeries, sandwich shops, and other new uses for old buildings. One that needs no renovation is Rankin's, in a plain cinderblock building at 2200 N. Central but arguably Knoxville's oldest continuously open restaurant, an old-school diner there since about 1950 and popular at breakfast and lunch today.

North Hills

North Hills, east of Broadway, boasted hills higher in altitude than those of Sequoyah Hills and Holston Hills, and offered a slightly more modest option for a commuter neighborhood. One of its longtime residents was millionaire grocer, broadcaster, and country-music promoter Cas Walker; Dolly Parton was especially fond of the eccentric old "coon hunter" who lived in a surprisingly modest house on Gaston Street, on a hillside where he could see his homeland, Sevier County. Artist Lloyd Branson, Knoxville's first full-time professional artist, was a bit of a vagabond much of his life, but in his later years settled on the edge of the neighborhood in a house on what's now called Branson Street.

THE BIRDHOUSE ON N FOURTH AVE

BUFFAT MILL *references one of several* FRENCH-SWISS FAMILIES *who settled here after* 1848

Part of North Hills, by the way, was originally a park established by Knoxville's German-immigrant community and called Turner Park—not for anyone named Turner, but for the *Turn Verein*, the German cultural organization.

North Knoxville is a patchwork of historic neighborhoods, most of them reviving through the efforts of residents with an interest in preserving the neighborhood's historic fabric.

To the north of Old North, on the west side of Broadway, are **OAKWOOD** and **LINCOLN PARK**, established in the late 19th century between central Knoxville and Sharp's Ridge as "trolleyburbs," streetcar-connected subdivisions established just before the primacy of automobiles. Both have some valuable century-old architecture. Central to Oakwood are Fulton High School and St. Mary's Hospital, East Tennessee's first Catholic hospital established on a hill here in 1929. The original brick building is still intact, but obscured by modern additions.

On the east side of Broadway are **EDGEWOOD, BELLE MORRIS** (a neighborhood named for an elementary school named for a beloved public-education pioneer who lived on Broadway) and

LINCOLN PARK HOME OWNERSHIP AD, *KNOXVILLE JOURNAL & TRIBUNE*, 1903

FAIRMONT-EMORILAND, early 1920s developments that were among Knoxville's first to be advertised as residential-only.

For the most part, these are purely residential neighborhoods with few public attractions except along Broadway's commercial strip. Some points along Broadway have historical interest, including the mid-century modern Fountain Lanes at 3315 N. Broadway, the bowling alley little changed since it opened in 1961.

To the north, **WHITTLE SPRINGS** is a little different, a mostly automobile-era neighborhood in the general vicinity of a once-stylish resort hotel that included an enormous swimming pool and a ballroom that hosted jazz-age dances—and later, a futuristic broadcasting studio with seating for 1,000. Although it closed by degrees and was demolished, Whittle Springs left one substantial trace, in the still-popular Whittle Springs Golf Course.

---

*F*OUNTAIN *C*ITY

Fountain City, at the end of Broadway near Knoxville's northern city limits, is defined by the valley between Sharp's Ridge and Black Oak Ridge. Though never a "city" with its own government, it always seemed a place apart from the rest of Knoxville. In fact, it wasn't even annexed into the city until 1962, after years of lawsuits attempting to block incorporation, and Fountain City greeted that gesture with a mock funeral. Fountain City can still seem different today, but you may need to know where to look.

John Adair, the most prominent Irish immigrant among the Knoxville area's early settlers, and a signer to the 1796 constitution that formed the state of Tennessee, lived in a fortified compound along what's now Broadway.

NORTHSIDE NEIGHBORHOODS *display an eclectic pageant of* 1890s-1930s RESIDENTIAL ARCHITECTURE

SPRING AND HOTEL, FOUNTAIN CITY, CA. 1907

NEIGHBORHOODS

Once called the Fountainhead, Fountain City was named for the fact that water forming the source of First Creek—yes, the same broad, muddy tributary that flows like a small river through a large culvert in downtown Knoxville—springs from the bluff of Black Oak Ridge in what's now Fountain City Park, one of the city's prettiest parks. By the time of the Civil War, the Fountainhead had a reputation as an idyllic spot for religious revivals, or "camp meetings," beginning a reputation it long nurtured for both moral and natural cleanliness.

EARLY 20TH CENTURY POSTCARD, WHITTLE SPRINGS HOTEL POOL

Its beauty attracted developers who by the 1880s were building the Fountainhead Hotel here, as a "springs resort." The hotel closed in the early 1900s, and later burned down. Only the name Hotel Avenue and the hotel's water feature, a heart-shaped pond, remain today. Whether you call it "the duck pond" or "Fountain City Lake" can start a good-natured argument.

Fountain City—as Fountainhead was renamed to avoid postal confusion with another Tennessee town—became a popular destination, both for northern tourists and for Knoxvillians, who could ride the small steam train that left hourly from downtown for the five-mile trek. The parkland along the creek was especially popular for Fourth of July and Labor Day events, including picnics, running races, and baseball games, which drew thousands.

Sometimes major speakers, like Socialist presidential candidate Eugene V. Debs, surprisingly popular in ca. 1900 Knoxville, spoke at Fountain City. (In fact, two of Debs' best-known speaking photographs were taken here.)

Once a TEMPERANCE HAVEN, *Fountain City still has* FEW BARS *per capita*

After the hotel closed, Fountain City emerged as a residential suburb, with little industry, and retained its reputation as a clean-living paradise noted for its dearth of both smoke and alcoholic beverages—each in stark contrast to downtown Knoxville—for most of the 20th century. Fountain City has been the home of several major community leaders, notably Harvey Broome, early supporter of the Great Smoky Mountains National Park, and a co-founder of the national Wilderness Society.

Union County native Roy Acuff moved here with his family as a teenager, and he became an aggressive athletic star at Central High long before he learned to play the fiddle (according to the story, a Fountain City auto mechanic showed him the basics). Stardom was long in coming, though, and Acuff was often in trouble with the law and rival bootleggers. He was once shot in a Hotel Avenue speakeasy. By 1935, he was becoming a revolutionary star in local radio, creating a new sensation of what had previously been known as "hillbilly music."

Today, it may take more imagination to see Fountain City as a paradise, beyond the traffic and corporate signage, but its spirit lives in Fountain City Park, the heart-shaped pond, and the friendly crowds at Litton's, a

SAVAGE GARDEN

grocery that evolved into a restaurant, and is now an institution. All those are within a walkable cluster. The rest of Fountain City may be most easily seen from the window of a car. It contains several handsome early 20th century homes of the Craftsman era.

One extraordinary feature of Fountain City, visible from the road and only occasionally open to the public, is the privately owned "oriental garden" known as Savage Gardens, on Garden Drive off Broadway. Established around 1917 by British-born industrialist Arthur Savage, it reflects its era's fascination with Asian styles. It lapsed into near-ruin after Savage's 1946 death, but its owner has worked to restore it in recent years. It's used by the adjacent Montessori school.

FOUNTAIN CITY LAKE, AKA "THE DUCK POND"

CENTRAL *was once Knox County's high school for* STUDENTS *who lived* OUTSIDE CITY LIMITS

SWAN'S BAKERY, MAGNOLIA AVE, 1934

EAST

East Knoxville comprises the neighborhoods on either side of its main artery, Magnolia Avenue. Today it's lined by more than 100 magnolia trees, but it's actually named for Magnolia Branner, a wealthy planter's widow who was mother of a Knoxville mayor, and who lived on this stylish street. Because it led to Chilhowee Park, it became the route of Knoxville's first electric streetcar, laid out in 1890 (by future U.S. Treasury Secretary William Gibbs McAdoo).

Over the years, Magnolia has been the address of Swan's Bakery (1927) and Catholic High School (1930), as well as several unusual restaurants, like the Pizza Palace (1960), which once catered to families headed to and from the park. In 1946, 1925 Magnolia was home to an enterprising soft-drink bottler that came up with the first recipe for Mountain Dew, originally formulated as a mixer for moonshine. Parts of Magnolia appear in the 1996 John Turturro-Sam Rockwell film, *Box of Moonlight*.

PARKRIDGE

Parkridge is another modern (1970s) designation for a reviving historic neighborhood that was originally considered to be part of something else. Much of what we know as East Knoxville was called Park City in the late 1800s. It drew its name from the fact that it lay between downtown and one of Knoxville's most celebrated attractions, Chilhowee Park. By 1917, another park at the neighborhood's western edge added to the agreeable theme, with the opening of Caswell Park, Knoxville's baseball field *(see p.149)*. Meanwhile, Chestnut Ridge, along the neighborhood's northern slope, was a mostly black community.

A combination of Park City and Chestnut Ridge, Parkridge is a neighborhood of mostly wooden Victorian houses. In fact, it holds America's highest concentration of homes designed by George Barber (1854–1915), a nationally known designer of fancy but still affordable Victorian or Queen Anne style houses. Originally from the Chicago area, he moved to Knoxville in 1888, where he made most of his career and became Knoxville's best-known architect.

SWAN'S *sponsored the nationally influential 1940s black gospel group* SWAN SILVERTONES

Barber lived in the part of Park City now known as Parkridge, and here created plans for his mail-order architecture business that resulted in houses across America.

Today, America has hundreds, perhaps thousands of George Barber Victorian houses, from New England to the Pacific Northwest, most of which the architect never saw in person. (His talented son, Charles Barber, grew up in Parkridge; with a style distinctly different from his father's, Charles co-founded the firm of Barber-McMurry, which thrives today.) Although Parkridge includes a lot of lovely early 20th century homes, most of Barber's Victorians are along Washington and Jefferson Avenues. The Barbers lived at 1635 Washington Avenue.

Rocked by the urban-renewal displacements, white flight, and interstate construction in the 1950s and '60s, Parkridge began reviving by degrees later in the century, with the landmark renovation of Park Place, a large, abandoned 1927 public school that became a cluster of condos in 1987. Today, Parkridge is a mixed-race neighborhood treading a careful line between effective preservation and the excesses of gentrification.

FORMER PARK CITY BRANCH LIBRARY

𝓕ive 𝓟oints

Underlying Parkridge on the map, south of Magnolia along Martin Luther King Boulevard, is Five Points, a term still used despite the fact that its five points were

THE PIZZA PALACE, A RARE PIZZA DRIVE-IN, DATES BACK TO 1960

"improved" away into rectangular blocks years ago. That area is central to East Knoxville's working-class black community, not far from the anchor of Austin-East High School. Restaurants like Jackie's Dream, at 2223 McCalla Ave., keep the neighborhood's soul-food heritage alive.

It was originally a predominantly white neighborhood, and during the '30s and early '40s, it was the home of a talented young actress named Patricia Neal, who lived on Linden Avenue and later Parkview. She got her first rave newspaper review when she was only 15, in a 1941 production of "Penny Wise" at the nearby Park Junior High. Her movie career would earn her two Oscars.

Louise Avenue was the home of blues legend Ida Cox (1893–1967), famous for her own song, "Wild Women Don't Have the Blues." She spent the last 20 years of her life in this neighborhood, during which she made one last record album.

The Riverside Drive and Dandridge Avenue areas include several historic houses, some of them on acreage that belonged to the once-powerful Williams family. John Williams (1778–1837) was an officer in the War of 1812, then a U.S. senator, then an ambassador to Central America. His final home, a brick house that's one of Knoxville's oldest, still stands at 2351 Dandridge Ave., at the head of the Williams Creek Golf Course. His son, who was also a prominent politician known as Col. John Williams, lived nearby, on Riverside, in another privately owned house that still exists. Both were ancestors of the playwright Tennessee Williams, whose father grew up in Knoxville.

JAMES AND ETHEL BECK

Tree-shaded Dandridge Avenue is also the address of the antebellum Mabry-Hazen House at 1711 Dandridge Ave. (*see p.32*) and the Beck Cultural Exchange Center at 1927 Dandridge Ave., the former home of African-American leaders James and Ethel Beck, early local leaders of the NAACP (*see p.38*). The 1912 house was a target of racist demonstrations when a black doctor moved into the previously white neighborhood in 1947; the Becks lived there later, and willed it to be used for celebrating African-American culture. Next door to the east is a home once owned by the family who produced artists Beauford and Joseph Delaney, and visited by both of them in their later years (*see p.39*).

Holston Hills

Founded in 1925 along the Holston River, the especially lovely small river that helps form the Tennessee, Holston Hills was one of Knoxville's first automobile-oriented subdivisions. Most of its houses are pretty, several featuring unusual stonework, but otherwise conservative for the era. One major exception is the 1943 house at 4215 Holston Hills Drive, designed by German-born Bauhaus alumnus Alfred Clauss, the first modernist architect to do substantial work in Knoxville.

Holston Hills boasts a couple of features Sequoyah Hills lacks: its own country club, with 1927 clubhouse, and a riverside golf course—designed by Scottish-born golfing guru Donald Ross, and often listed as one of America's "classic" courses.

Burlington

Not far from Holston Hills, near Chilhowee Park, is an older community called Burlington, which has struggled over the years, and no longer has a soda fountain and a movie theater. But some semblance of its old downtown survives along Martin Luther King, with a classic barber shop, a couple of specialty restaurants, and an eccentric flea market. It was once the eastern terminus of the electric streetcar, which was especially busy during Chilhowee Park's heyday. In recent years, a few renovations in Burlington have pointed toward some hope of revival.

FORMER SCHOOL FOR THE DEAF FOR BLACK STUDENTS AT WILLIAMS CREEK GOLF COURSE

To date, the ORIGIN *of the name* BURLINGTON *remains a* MYSTERY

"KNAFFL HOUSE" ON SPEEDWAY CIRCLE

Burlington's rarity, though, is an especially peculiar neighborhood called Speedway Circle. Its street, oval in shape, has houses on either side. It was, from the 1890s until about 1920, Cal Johnson's Racetrack. A horse-racing track established by a well-respected former slave, the half-mile oval track suffered from the statewide banning of betting, but in the 1910s, it cheered some of Knoxville's first automobile races. It was also the site of the first aeroplane landing in town, in 1910, hosted by elderly Cal Johnson himself.

CAL JOHNSON

Have a close look at the unusual brick house, shaded with trees on the north side of the track. Older than any other house on the street, the former home of pioneer photographer Joseph Knaffl once stood on Gay Street until it—or the front part of it—was moved here in the 1920s. Although stripped of much of its interior furnishings, it's occasionally the subject of a renovation proposal.

SOUTH

South Knoxville was mostly rural and industrial—thick woods pocked with marble quarries and lumber mills—and largely ignored by mainstream Knoxville until the 1920s, when excitement about the suddenly accessible Smoky Mountains drew new traffic. Upon its completion in the early 1930s, Chapman Highway, which leads toward Sevierville, became the nation's main route to the Great Smoky Mountains National Park. It's named for Col. David Chapman, the South Knoxvillian remembered as the Park's "father." Although there are now faster highways to the Smokies, Chapman Highway remains South Knoxville's main artery, roughly bisecting the section. Today, Chapman Highway offers traces of its tourist years, along with an ever-changing variety of restaurants and shops.

Because of its perceived remoteness, South Knoxville was once derided as "South America." Not only was it across the river, but its topography was rugged and unfamiliar. Then and now, that became a source of brash pride. Of course, it's no longer really remote, connected by Chapman Highway and Alcoa Highway, which leads not just to the industrial aluminum town of its name but to McGhee Tyson Airport. Some prefer older Maryville Pike, a slower and more picturesque route to that county seat, home of Maryville College.

However, not far off these major arteries are narrow, twisty roads through wooded hills. With a few single-lane trestle underpasses, some roads seem like remote mountain roads, even though they may be hardly a mile from downtown. Only recently has the city begun to capitalize on South Knoxville's persistent wildness as an asset. Today, dozens of miles of walking and biking trails connecting park attractions are part of what's called the Urban Wilderness.

CHAPMAN HIGHWAY *and the Smokies' lofty* MOUNT CHAPMAN *both honor the same South Knoxvillian*

PEREZ DICKINSON'S ISLAND HOME ESTATE, CA. 1880S

NEIGHBORHOODS

Island Home

South Knoxville's best-known historic neighborhood is called Island Home. (Those who live in the historic core still use the developer's original name, Island Home Park.) Not actually on an island, but along a river shore near central Knoxville's largest island, Island Home got its name from Massachusetts-born Perez Dickinson, a cousin of the poet Emily. Dickinson purchased both the island—Dickinson Island, now home of the Downtown Island Airport—and hundreds of acres along the river shore near it. Here he built his "Island Home," a brick house that served as the headquarters for his impressive experimental farm and as a sort of sociable refuge. That house still stands on the campus of the Tennessee School for the Deaf. That public K-12 institution for the hearing impaired, one of the oldest such schools in America, moved here in the 1920s. Offering services to 200–300 students from across the state, TSD uses Perez Dickinson's old brick house for administrative offices.

The Island Home Park neighborhood sprang up around 1911, along Island Home Boulevard (Knoxville's first street to be designated as a "boulevard," by the way). It was such a popular residential option that it earned its own electric streetcar from downtown. Today it's especially well known for its Craftsman-style houses. Among Island Home's children are Tony-winning Broadway and TV star John Cullum, who grew up here. Arthur Morgan, the first and most revolutionary chairman of the Tennessee Valley Authority, lived there as he was planning the construction of Norris Dam, along with his perfect company town, Norris, designed as a model for an ideal community. Pulitzer-winning investigative journalist Paul Y. Anderson (1893–1938), credited for his exposure of the Teapot Dome Scandal, also grew up nearby, and is buried under an unusually stylish stone at Island Home Baptist Church.

ISLAND HOME EARLY 1900S POSTCARD

The head of the TENNESSEE RIVER *is just a greenway* BIKE RIDE *from* ISLAND HOME

ISLAND HOME BLVD

It's an unusual neighborhood today, across one little strand of the river from Dickinson Island. It has its own riverfront park, but Island Home is also near Ijams Nature Center, the 300-acre park that began more than a century ago as a semi-private bird sanctuary (*see p.154*), which itself is linked to many miles of bike trails throughout much of South Knoxville.

STONE PILLARS AT THE ENTRANCE TO ISLAND HOME PARK COMMUNITY

Leading in that direction is once-industrial Sevier Avenue. Ignored by the city for years, Sevier is lately blooming with cafés and craft-beer attractions in pre-war buildings, along with new, riverside Suttree Landing Park. There is new life in the Baker Creek area (at the southern end of hard-to-follow Sevier Avenue). In the general neighborhood is Stanley's Greenhouse, a family-owned institution since 1955.

Other south-side neighborhoods of historic interest include **LINDBERGH FOREST**, a tree-shaded pre-war subdivision just to the south of Island Home. (Yes, it was named for the daring pilot, at the height of his fame, in 1927, as the result of a newspaper contest.) On the other side of Chapman Highway is unpretentious **VESTAL**, an old working-man's community within walking distance of a lumber yard by that name, but also including the old Candoro building, a marble company's 1924 headquarters whose marble construction mimics an Italian villa. Its

CANDORO ARTS & HERITAGE CENTER

REGAL CINEMAS *recently established its* GLOBAL HEADQUARTERS *on the south bank* annual festival—called, of course, Vestival—is part church picnic, part hippie Happening.

Maybe it's the rough topography, but South Knoxville conceals multiple anomalies. One of them is **LOGHAVEN**, a log-cabin community near Cherokee Bluffs, established by a single mother in the 1930s as a source of income. It's soon to be an artist residency, hosting musicians, painters, authors, and even choreographers for limited stays.

Between there and UT Hospital is the Body Farm, an internationally known forensic research center for the study of corpse decomposition, primarily for criminal-investigation purposes. More than one mystery novel has used the facility as a setting, including Patricia Cornwell's 1994 bestseller, *The Body Farm*.

A dead-end street just off Chapman Highway is called **LITTLE SWITZERLAND**. It was an all-modernist community conceived in the 1930s by German immigrant and Bauhaus alumnus Alfred Clauss and his wife Jane, also an accomplished architect. The flat-roofed, big-windowed houses would have seemed "ultramodern" as late as the 1960s—but in the '30s and '40s, they were shocking. The Clausses, who did significant modernist work in Philadelphia and elsewhere, lived in Little Switzerland for several years.

ALFRED CLAUSS-DESIGNED HOUSE ON LITTLE SWITZERLAND

And the rugged hilltops bear the ruins of three Civil War forts, two of them easily accessible *(see p.96)*.

South Knoxville has produced many interesting Americans, including Hollywood "Jackass" Johnny Knoxville and novelist Cormac McCarthy, who spent his adolescent years in a rural home at the corner of circuitous Martin Mill Pike and Artella Drive. The house is described in his Pulitzer-winning novel, *The Road*, but—not out of character with one of his novels—his empty house attracted vagrants, and burned down in 2009.

LOGHAVEN CABIN

LOGHAVEN *was once home to the publishers of* ESQUIRE MAGAZINE

KNOXVILLE COLLEGE, FOUNDED 1875

WEST

West Knoxville grew explosively in the 50 years after World War II, much of that along a 1790s route known as Kingston Pike. The road to Kingston, county seat of Roane County, it was long the first leg of the trip to Nashville, but also a semi-rural residential address for families, several of them affluent. By 1920, the old road served as a junction of two national routes, the Dixie and Lee Highways, leading from the upper Midwest to Florida, and from Washington to New Orleans, respectively. For decades, much of the Pike's business was tourist-related, motor courts and eye-catching restaurants. Today, it's East Tennessee's most commercial 15-mile strip, but if you look beyond the chain-franchise signage, you can see glimpses of the past, like a few antebellum houses and mid-century motels now used for other purposes. The best-preserved historic part of Kingston Pike is the tree-shaded mile just west of UT, between Neyland Drive and Lyons View, which includes several century-old brick homes. With only a few exceptions, most of Kingston Pike past there is emblematic of America's commercial sprawl, though a few spots, like Homberg Place and Bearden Hill, make interesting exceptions. West Town Mall (1972), the region's first covered shopping mall, is still in business at Kingston Pike and Morrell Road.

Other westerly routes include 19th-century Middlebrook Pike, just to the north of I-40—it has no particular destination, but empties into the Pellissippi Parkway area—and Western Avenue, which angles to the north just enough to become Oak Ridge Highway, the World War II-era route that connects to the once-famous Atomic City.

MECHANICSVILLE

Knoxville's oldest neighborhood outside of downtown—just across Second Creek on the northwestern corner of the original urban area—Mechanicsville is named for the "mechanics" who worked at the Knoxville Iron Works, Knoxville's biggest employer in the years just after the Civil War. The factory's 1871 "Foundry," part of the original plant, still thrives on World's Fair Park as an event space.

Mechanicsville began as a mixed-race community of African-Americans and Welsh

Commercial and residential WEST KNOXVILLE *sprawls* 20 MILES WEST *of* DOWNTOWN

immigrants who built many of the wooden houses that form the older part of the neighborhood in the years just after the Civil War.

As surprising as it may seem, English-born author Frances Hodgson Burnett, famous for *The Secret Garden* and *Little Lord Fauntleroy*, published her first several short stories when she was a teenager living in a small cottage she called "Noah's Ark" on a hillside overlooking Mechanicsville in 1868.

FRANCES HODGSON BURNETT, CA. 1908

Later, in 1875, part of Mechanicsville became the campus of Knoxville College. Originally a Presbyterian teachers' college for former slaves, it evolved into a nationally respected four-year college for blacks. It drew visits from major national figures, including Frederick Douglass, Booker T. Washington, W.E.B. Dubois, Jesse Owens, and Martin Luther King, who in 1960 spoke to a crowd of thousands on its lawn, helping inspire peaceful—and successful—desegregationist actions in Knoxville.

Like many historically black colleges, KC began having problems with enrollment in the late 20th century. It has been completely closed since 2015, and although there remain hopes that it may reopen someday, its deteriorating campus has been the subject of proposed redevelopment. Its associated cemetery, along College Street is known as Freedmen's Mission Cemetery, and holds the graves of many prominent blacks, among them James and Ethel Beck *(see p.38)*, and former slaves of Andrew Johnson. A slaveholding Unionist, Johnson was becoming a national figure, unexpectedly soon to be president, when he freed his slaves during the Civil War. That gesture is believed to have inspired the annual celebration of Emancipation Day on August 8, a date celebrated in East Tennessee and few other places.

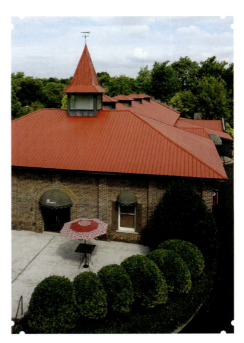

THE FOUNDRY (1871) IS NOW AN EVENT SPACE

JAMES AND ETHEL BECK GRAVESTONE AT FREEDMEN'S MISSION CEMETERY ADJACENT TO KNOXVILLE COLLEGE

By the 1930s, Mechanicsville was home to a nightclub called Neal's Savoy. The club at University and College brought in some major jazz stars like pianist Earl Hines and bandleader Fletcher Henderson to play for biracial but segregated audiences.

MECHANICSVILLE FIRE HALL

Mechanicsville was deteriorating badly before the 1970s, when it became the subject of a concerted preservationist effort that continues. Today, Mechanicsville features some of the finest Victorian architecture in the Knoxville area—along with two of Knoxville's three wedge-shaped "flatiron" brick commercial buildings, all ca. 1902. The large old 1930 Moses School survives as home of a police station and religious academy.

Although it still has problems, it's today a mostly beautiful mixed-race neighborhood with athletic fields and, at 419 Arthur Street, Knoxville's most picturesque old fire hall, in operation since 1909. A downtown section still supports a barbershop, barbecue, and offices along University Avenue at College Street.

In the 20th century, the low-lying western extension of the community became known as McAnally Flats. Much of its residential housing stock was destroyed with interstate highway construction by the 1960s, and the term is rarely used today. But the phrase enjoyed a revival of sorts when novelist Cormac McCarthy referred to McAnally Flats repeatedly in his darkly comic 1979 narrative, *Suttree*, set in the 1950s. Definitions of where Mechanicsville ended and McAnally Flats began vary with the teller and perhaps the decade, but McAnally Flats has been described as the mostly inexpensive and heavily African-American residential area to the south and west of Western Avenue.

LONSDALE

Just to the north of Mechanicsville is Lonsdale, a hilly and traditionally mixed-race community clustered around Tennessee's only steel mill. Most of its modest working-man's homes date to the early 20th century, and Lonsdale still retains remnants of a downtown that once had restaurants, fraternal lodges, and a movie theater. Novelist David Madden (b. 1933) grew up here. When he submitted a novel set in Lonsdale, it confused editors who thought he'd made this place up—no place, they said, can be so urban and so rural at the same time. (After he simplified the setting, placing it in Kentucky instead, *Cassandra Singing* became his most-praised novel.)

J.T. MOORE "FLAT IRON" BUILDING (1902)

LONSDALE'S STREETS *combine names of* STATES *and* CIVIL WAR GENERALS

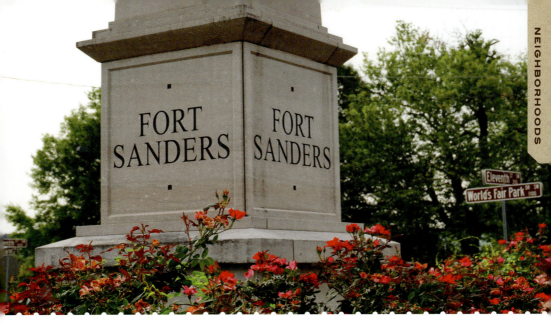

Lonsdale keeps to itself, off all beaten paths, just east of Western Avenue, and mostly out of sight. Next to Tennessee's only steel mill is extraordinary Racheff Gardens, a beautiful if sometimes noisy gated flower garden established in 1947 by the plant's co-owner, Bulgarian immigrant Ivan Racheff, who was very proud of what he created here (*see p.147*).

Fort Sanders

Fort Sanders is Knoxville's most famous neighborhood. Straddling a ridge north of Cumberland Avenue immediately to the west of downtown, it took its name from the area's largest Union fort, named for Gen. William Sanders, who died during the Confederate siege of Knoxville (*see p.91*). The earthworks stood along the crest of the ridge between what's now 16th and 18th Streets, and became a tourist attraction, central to the unusual "Blue-Gray Reunion" of 1890. By 1920, its last remnants had yielded to residential development. (Whether its outline is still discernible in the topography of lawns is a matter of debate.) A large marble Union monument stands at the corner of 16th Street and Clinch Avenue, showing soldiers reconciling. A smaller Confederate monument stands on 17th Street near Laurel Avenue, near the spot where 129 soldiers died in a desperate attack on the fort's steep ramparts on Nov. 29, 1863.

Originally known as West End, the neighborhood attracted the affluent and their architects in the 1880s and 1890s. Only a few of the larger houses survive.

An array of creative people have enjoyed Fort Sanders as a setting for their youths, so many that you might conclude the neighborhood itself had some influence.

Anne Armstrong (1873–1958), a pioneer female business executive and sometime novelist—*The Seas of God* was a transatlantic sensation for at least a moment in 1915—spent her teen years on Clinch Avenue in the 1880s, and remembered them in a vivid memoir called "Of Time and Knoxville." Impressionist artist Catherine Wiley (1879–1958) grew up in Fort Sanders, and as an adult did much of her best work in a studio on White Avenue.

FORT SANDERS *was briefly incorporated* (1888-1897) *as* "WEST KNOXVILLE"

Philosopher, critic, author, and maverick environmentalist Joseph Wood Krutch (1893–1969) grew up in the southeastern edge of Fort Sanders. Bernadotte Schmitt (1886–1969) was a Rhodes Scholar whose book *The Coming of War, 1914* won the Pulitzer Prize for History; he grew up in a house on White Avenue, near Catherine Wiley's studio.

CATHERINE WILEY, CA. 1900

Most famously, James Agee (1909–1955) remembered Fort Sanders in his prose poem "Knoxville: Summer 1915," which became internationally famous first when it was used in composer Samuel Barber's similarly titled soprano piece, "Knoxville: Summer of 1915." Agee later drew on his memories of youth in Fort Sanders and the automobile wreck that killed his father in his Pulitzer-winning novel *A Death in the Family*, which was adapted into a Pulitzer-winning Broadway play as well as four motion pictures. The first of them, *All the Way Home*, starring Robert Preston and Jean Simmons, was shot in the neighborhood in 1963. Ironically, Agee's home, in the 1500 block of Highland, was torn down just as the movie was being planned.

UNTITLED (MOTHER AND CHILD IN MEADOW), 1913 BY CATHERINE WILEY

In the early 1920s, the Presbyterian church established a modest-sized hospital that used the name of the nearby fort. Meanwhile, the University of Tennessee, originally confined to its Hill, was growing rapidly, and as early as the 1920s, some old family houses in the neighborhood were being adapted as boarding houses for students. Both the hospital and the university have grown exponentially since then, and still vie for acreage in Fort Sanders, often at the expense of its historic homes.

JAMES AGEE

West End became more commonly known as Fort Sanders in the 1950s, with the establishment of Fort Sanders Elementary School. By then, much of the neighborhood was becoming known as a "student ghetto," a lively and attractive if run-down sort of semi-bohemian neighborhood. (Agee, a bohemian's bohemian, became more famous after his sudden death in 1955, adding to the mystique.)

Even as the neighborhood changed, it continued to nurture the artistic impulse. A university artist in residence, Marion Greenwood (1909–1970), associate of Diego Rivera, moved into a studio on Clinch Avenue at 19th Street in 1954, and created her famous and sometimes controversial mural, "The History of Tennessee." Horror-fantasy writer Karl Wagner (1945–1994) lived here and used the neighborhood as a setting for some early short stories.

Several rock bands that made a national splash began rehearsing in Fort Sanders rental houses. Songwriter R.B. Morris (b. 1952), later Knoxville's first official poet laureate, lived in Fort Sanders for decades, and evokes the neighborhood in his work.

In the 1980s, cartoonist Lowell Cunningham (b. 1959) lived in the neighborhood, and by his own account was inspired to create "The Men in Black" series

1967 | *New York photographer* **DANNY LYON** *published a series focused on* **FORT SANDERS**

THE ROSS MANSION, LAUREL TERRACE (1894), ON LAUREL AVE

by a nocturnal walk around Fort Sanders. His graphic-novel series inspired the movies about those characters.

In 1999, 15th Street became James Agee Street; soon after, the city developed Agee Park, a pocket of green at the corner of Laurel Avenue, about a block from Agee's home *(see p.156)*.

Today, much of Fort Sanders' original Victorian feel has evaporated, as Queen Anne houses have yielded to concrete apartment buildings and parking lots. However, several notable houses still stand. Laurel Terrace is a businessman's 1894 brick mansion at 1415 Laurel. Union veteran, sometime mayor, and influential editor William Rule lived his later years at 1604 Clinch.

Laurel Theater, originally a 1898 Presbyterian church, is now a lively performance space run by Jubilee Community Arts. Perhaps Fort Sanders' oldest building is the 1870s "Gardener's Cottage," at the corner of White Avenue and 16th. Originally home to a British gardener who created the impressive grounds of the Cowan Mansion (torn down decades ago), the Gardener's Cottage has recently been refurbished for new uses by the university.

In spite of the changes that make parts of the neighborhood look more ordinary than it used to seem, a walk around Fort Sanders is still an interesting way to spend an afternoon.

The Strip

West Cumberland Avenue from the 1600 block at the top of the hill to the trestle at the bottom, "the Strip" thrives between UT's campus and Fort Sanders, drawing energy from both. It was a commercial area by the 1920s, featuring restaurants, shops, and even a movie theater. Here daring restaurants introduced Italian, Mexican, and other cuisines to the city. (The world's first Ruby Tuesday opened on the Strip in 1972.)

Counterculture sorts were calling it "the Strip" by the late 1960s; the term became more widely known to the public when it became the target of an enormous 1971 drug bust. The word took on a new meaning in early 1974, during the streaking craze, when hundreds of people shucked their clothes in public here. The Strip was well known for live music, especially during the hippie and punk eras. Bands from REM to Black Flag played in bars on the Strip in the early '80s. Slowly it lost much of its distinctive character to chain stores and parking lots, but a recent city initiative to re-introduce urban architecture promises to restore some of its liveliness.

Author **NORMAN MAILER** *once* **ARM-WRESTLED** *challengers at a Forest Avenue bar*

CHEROKEE BLVD
INDIAN MOUND

Sequoyah Hills

The neighborhood once most associated with old money, is also, arguably, the city's most public neighborhood. Sequoyah Hills includes Cherokee Boulevard, a favorite walking and jogging path (and always a key part of the annual Knoxville Marathon), as well as a broad expanse of riverfront parkland, with hundreds of acres of mown grass, some interesting paths through copses of trees, a boat launch, and perhaps Knoxville's closest

SEQUOYAH SCHOOL (1929)

approximation of a beach. As early as the 1930s, it was a notorious place for lovers to "spoon." On summer afternoons today, you might find volleyball, horseshoes, bocce ball, and lots of dogs.

This river peninsula was known from the 1790s as Looney's Bend—that label still appears on riverboatmen's charts, and for barges, it remains one of the river's most hazardous turns. Sequoyah Hills developed in 1925 as one of Knoxville's first automobile suburbs—one of the first generation of neighborhoods designed for people who didn't necessarily have to walk to work or catch a streetcar. Cherokee Boulevard, a little more than three miles long, follows the outer contour of the peninsula. Roughly in the middle, the boulevard's median widens to make way for the worn remnant of an Indian mound, which may have suggested the Native American theme for the neighborhood— although the mound builders preceded the Cherokee by several centuries.

For a short time after its first development, Sequoyah Hills coexisted with a daringly different development. The Boulevard includes several unusual concrete features— a pool, a fenced enclosure, an obelisk with panther heads. Unveiled in 1926 as Talahi, it was to be a planned town-center

Although spelled differently, CALIFORNIA'S SEQUOIA REDWOODS *are named for the same* CHEROKEE LEADER

VINTAGE TALAHI DR POSTCARD

The local legend that Sequoyah (1767–1843), the Cherokee scholar who created the first American alphabet, had something to do with this peninsula isn't supported by facts. Sequoyah was born along the Little Tennessee River, about 35 miles southwest of Knoxville. He may have visited Knoxville as a youth, but never lived here, and left Tennessee in middle age, eventually settling in the West.

However, the neighborhood named for him has been home to a motley variety of other famous Americans including, briefly, some talented teenagers: Patricia Neal, the Oscar-winning actress earned her first acting notices, and began her career as a pro, as a teenager living with her struggling parents in a small apartment in Sequoyah Village in the early '40s; and the Everly Brothers, who discovered rock'n'roll when they lived with their own parents in a boarding house on Scenic Drive in the mid-'50s.

Later, *Roots* author Alex Haley lived in a large house on Cherokee Boulevard for a few years in the 1980s, and Pulitzer Prize-winning war reporter Don Whitehead lived in an apartment here in retirement. Future governor Bill Haslam grew up in Sequoyah Hills, and spent much of that time playing baseball on the Polo Field.

community in which personal property was de-emphasized with a ban on fences and an enforced respect for the natural environment. Binding it together was a theme that combined Cherokee imagery, like the Thunderbird, with crypto-Eqyptian and art-deco themes. The idea was that people would live here and walk to a town-center commercial cluster, and to athletic fields along the river. It was a commercial disappointment, though, even before the Depression's arrival decisively ended the idyll. Its idealistic planner committed suicide.

But Talahi left some lovely features, and that proposed town center did support a cluster of stores near old-fashioned apartment buildings. Today, Sequoyah is home to only a few multi-millionaires, but many affluent professionals, and hundreds of UT students who rent houses or apartments here. The riverfront field, originally envisioned as a polo grounds, rarely served that purpose, but is best known today for Little League baseball.

OBELISK WITH PANTHER FOUNTAIN ADJACENT TO PAPOOSE PARK AT TALAHI DR AND TALILUNA AVE

EGYPTIAN SYMBOLS *became popular after the* 1922 DISCOVERY *of* KING TUT'S TOMB

Bearden

Bearden today is an amalgam of about a mile and a half of trafficky, commercial Kingston Pike; the affluent residential riverbluff known as Lyons View; the region's oldest country club and golf course; a modest African-American neighborhood; East Tennessee's only Catholic cathedral; and a riverside park that was once a mental institution.

A semi-rural community for many years before it was annexed into Knoxville in 1962, Bearden once had its own train station but never its own city limits. Its boundaries vary with the person describing it, but all definitions center it around the intersection of Kingston Pike and Northshore. The Bearden depot was once there, and Fourth Creek, along Northshore, bisects the neighborhood north and south.

Some residents and merchants would stretch the concept of Bearden east to Sequoyah Hills or West High School. Some would stretch it to the west to about Morrell Road, to include the neighborhoods of West Hills and Westmoreland. Complicating the

BEARDEN MEMORIAL IN HIGHLAND CEMETERY

issue is that in the 1970s, Bearden High moved a good two miles west of the original neighborhood of Bearden, but kept the name.

Originally including an Irish-dominant neighborhood called Erin, Bearden got its name in the late 19th century not from a bear den, but through its association with mayor, sheriff, and state legislator Marcus DeLafayette Bearden, the younger. (Strange as it may seem, there were two by that name; they were cousins, and the elder was responsible for the 19th-century paper mill on Third Creek from which Papermill Road

KINGSTON PIKE LOOKING EAST FROM BEARDEN HILL

FOURTH CREEK, *the last of Knoxville's named creeks, is central to Bearden* got its name.) That younger Bearden worked to establish the Lyons View Asylum, a state mental institution that became the area's biggest employer. Today, the old "asylum" is popular Lakeshore Park (*see p.156*).

Knoxville's first commercial airport opened on Bearden's eastern fringe in the 1920s. By then the commerce of cross-country tourists along the old Dixie-Lee Highway, a junction of two major national routes along Kingston Pike, made Bearden a natural place for tourist courts, motels, "Southern-style" restaurants, beer joints, and even a couple of movie theaters (one of them a drive-in). It also developed some industry, including a brickyard and a hat factory (hence the name Homberg Place, a small, pedestrian-scale shopping center within Bearden).

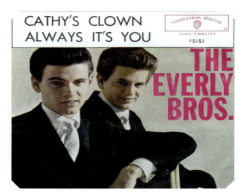

THE EVERY BROS. 1960 SINGLE

NAPLES, FORMERLY THE WAYSIDE INN

The construction of Interstates 40 and 75 bypassed all that in the 1960s, starving Bearden's tourist economy, but you can still see a few remnants of old Bearden in the modest scale of the existing buildings, the persistence of locally owned shops—and sidewalks. A few institutions remain from the tourist era, like Naples. The old-school Italian restaurant is little changed since the early 1960s, but before that it was a roadside attraction called the Wayside Inn. Long's Drugs, open since 1956, is one of the nation's few independent drugstores that still maintains its original soda fountain.

The neighborhood's oldest house stands on the summit of Bearden Hill. One of a small handful of antebellum homes still standing along Kingston Pike, Knollwood (1851) was a family residence for over a century, and served both as headquarters for Confederate generals during the siege of Knoxville in 1863 and, a half century later, the childhood home of a U.S. general. Bruce Holloway (1912–1999) was a successful fighter pilot during World War II who became a four-star general in the Air Force. He developed an interest in flying as a youth in Bearden, watching planes take off from the city's original airport on Sutherland Avenue.

Other notable Beardenites include soul singer Clifford Curry ("She Shot a Hole in My Soul"), who lived in the predominantly black community between Kingston Pike and Lyons View. A new park on Kingston Pike at Forest Park honors the Everly Brothers, who attended nearby West High when they began experimenting with rock'n'roll as a duo on local radio around 1955, separate from their parents' band. Their biggest American hit, "Cathy's Clown" is known to be based on a West High romance.

Near Everly Brothers Parks is the Ice Chalet, an old-fashioned ice-skating rink from about 1962 and little changed since the Kennedy administration, but still a popular evening and weekend diversion today.

1850s | LYONS VIEW *was the subject of* PAINTINGS *by Scottish artist* JAMES CAMERON

Thunder Road

Bearden's familiarity to cross-country travelers may be responsible for its surprise appearance in a pop song that has become a legend, and a favorite local mystery. Movie star Robert Mitchum, who had a passing acquaintance with East Tennessee through fishing trips—and who had briefly even worked with James Agee in the noir horror film *The Night of the Hunter*—created a movie of his own called *Thunder Road*, the tale of a Kentucky bootlegger. In the script, Knoxville is mentioned only a few times. The 1958 movie, a drive-in favorite well into the 1960s, seems to end with the bootlegger's fiery death in a car chase near Memphis. However, in the theme song, "The Ballad of Thunder Road," quoted briefly in the movie but released as a single with multiple stanzas, Bearden is central to the bootlegger's fate.

POSTER FOR THE 1957 MOVIE THUNDER ROAD STARRING ROBERT MITCHUM

*"Blazing right through Knoxville,
out on Kingston Pike
Then right outside of Bearden they made the fatal strike...."*

The catchy tune soared on Billbord's charts for an uncommonly long time between 1958 and 1962. It became hummably familiar to millions. That geographically specific couplet spawned legends, lies, serious books and articles, driving events, and a dozen plausible but perhaps unprovable stories about the "real" story of Thunder Road. Mitchum himself died in 1997 without ever revealing his inspiration. The fact that several bootleggers died in Knoxville-area police chases makes the song's origin, if indeed it was a true story, a challenge for historians.

Knoxville's answer to Hollywood Boulevard is an oddity beside a sidewalk along the 5100 block of Homberg Drive. In 1970, actress Ingrid Bergman was in town for the premier of her movie, *A Walk in the Spring Rain*, held at the Capri Cinema because the film had been partly shot in Knoxville. It was a big deal for Bearden, and Bergman obligingly signed her name and left her handprints in concrete outside the theater.

It became a trend, and other show-biz celebrities followed suit, including Patricia Neal, Cliff Robertson, Tippi Hedren and Stan Brock (who eventually moved to Knoxville). These concrete blocks outlasted the three movie theaters whose events attracted these stars.

On the western fringe of Bearden north of Kingston Pike, **WEST HILLS** was a model postwar subdivision, and is the setting of Knoxville's first modernist house to be listed on the National Register of Historic Places: Bruce McCarty's 1954 Hotpoint House at 509 West Hills Road, a house with a concrete core and cantilevered walls, was meant to be a national model for simplicity.

CAPRI 70 PREMIERE OF WALK IN THE SPRING RAIN WITH INGRID BERGMAN

RACE TRACK AT CONCORD FAIRGROUNDS, 1915

On the western fringe of West Hills is a very different historical site that reminds us that even in the most modern neighborhoods, the distant past lurks beneath the perfect green lawns. The site of **CAVETT'S STATION**, and the 1793 massacre that left 13 dead are said to be buried in a mass grave off Broome Road.

Less than a mile due north of Bearden is Middlebrook Pike, itself named for an antebellum house that still stands, but, privately owned and occupied, is almost invisible from the road. However, another historic structure, the Lones-Dowell house, is an approachable ca. 1858 farmhouse at 6341 Middlebrook Pike, home to one of the region's most prominent families, and now part of a respectfully configured business park that includes a small slave cemetery.

Just down the road is a longtime Knoxville institution, Wright's Cafeteria, at 5403 Middlebrook Pike. An oasis in the middle of an industrial/commercial strip, Wright's has hardly changed since it completed its evolution from a grocery store that was there in the 1950s. An occasional meal at the home-style lunch spot is still a political prerequisite for all office seekers.

Concord

Concord, an unincorporated community just beyond Knoxville's city limits to the west, is roughly the area around Concord Park, an almost nautical region alongside a broad part of Fort Loudoun Lake. Marinas, causeways, bait shops, and waterfront restaurants are part of the landscape around a lake so broad it can seem like a maritime bay, and often the wind can work up some almost ocean-like waves.

LONES-DOWELL HOUSE AT DOWELL SPRINGS

In the 1890s and early 1900s, the **CONCORD RACE TRACK** *was an* **ATTRACTION**

THE AVERY RUSSELL HOUSE / CAMPBELL STATION INN CA. 1898

The lake, an impoundment of the Tennessee River, has existed only since TVA completed Fort Loudoun Dam in 1943. But after more than 75 years, it seems as if it's been there forever, and thousands of locals have grown up in and around boats.

Old Concord intrigues visitors who can see it across the inlet from the park. In a suburban area where almost everything is new and aimed at the affluent, it's a secluded bit of 19th century America. Concord was a coherent rural community with its own railroad depot and post office by the 1850s, with an economy partly driven by nearby marble quarries. Concord's original street grid, and some of its historic homes, and commercial buildings—like the long-closed but still identified "BANK"—survive in the 21st century, but it's mainly a residential community with few specific attractions for visitors other than the Presbyterian church, the Masonic Lodge, and an art gallery or two.

THE OLD "BANK" ON FRONT ST IN CONCORD

Farragut

Enhancing the nautical theme is some deep and authentic history. This northern bank of

MOSTLY RURAL *until the* 1970s, SOUTHWESTERN KNOX COUNTY *has exploded in population*

the river was the first home of the U.S. Navy's first admiral, David Glasgow Farragut, the Union commander known for the famous order, "Damn the torpedoes! Full speed ahead!"

His father, Spanish immigrant Jordi (or George) Farragut-Mesquida, was a sailor who came to America mainly to fight the British during the Revolutionary War. He was an old salt who had sailed several seas when he settled here to operate a ferry across the river, and it was here that his son, the future admiral, was born in 1801.

ADMIRAL FARRAGUT

Farragut's actual birthplace, believed to be near the river's shore, was marked with some pageantry involving a flotilla of steamboats in 1900, led by Admiral Dewey. The marker was recently moved to Farragut Town Hall, as the result of a redevelopment, but the original site was immediately east of Northshore's Admiral Farragut Park.

The Farragut family left here, down the river for New Orleans. President Jefferson, having purchased Spanish Louisiana, called on patriotic Spanish speakers to help govern it. Farragut probably didn't return to Concord after his childhood, but this naval association—along with that of his transoceanic seaman father—folds in serendipitously with the boat-centered culture of Concord today. It's a more watery place now than the riverside home the Farraguts knew.

Just beyond Concord is Knox County's only other incorporated community. Farragut is an affluent suburban town previously known mainly as a historic spot called Campbell's Station. Named for the admiral, Farragut incorporated only in 1980, in part to prevent the rampant commercialism, especially in terms of signage, that characterizes much of Kingston Pike. Farragut is mostly a bedroom community not known for tourism, but has a few landmarks to note.

One is the old Campbell's Station building, known as the Avery Russell House, a brick Federal-style house of unknown age (variously estimated from 1795 to 1835, though recent scholarship has suggested it's ca. 1820) right on Kingston Pike. Campbell's Station existed here as a lodging place by the 1790s. (French botanist André Michaux visited ca. 1793—and, in his journal, mistook its name for Camel's Station!)

The remaining house, which may be the same building where President Andrew Jackson stayed in 1835—and where he encountered fellow tenant British geologist George Featherstonhaugh—is under redevelopment and may soon be reborn as an inn, returning to its original purpose. As is, it makes an interesting contrast with the modern commercial development along the far-western end of Kingston Pike.

Near the Avery-Russell House was the site of the 1863 Battle of Campbell Station (*see p.90*). To its south is Farragut Town Hall, a modern building for public meetings, but whose front yard includes what's surely the largest statue of Admiral Farragut south of Washington's Farragut Square.

THE AVERY RUSSELL HOUSE / CAMPBELL STATION INN TODAY

JORDI-FARRAGUT-MESQUIDA *was one of the most prominent* LATINO COMBATANTS *in the Revolutionary War*

KNOXVILLE BOTANICAL
GARDEN & ARBORETUM

PARKS & GARDENS

Well into the 20th century, the city bemoaned its dearth of parks. The city now has more than 90 individual parks, thousands of acres of public space in all, most of them created by local government, but a few run by private foundations. All these parks have stories, but below are several of unusual historical interest.

DOWNTOWN

 ### Krutch Park

Located at 504 Market Street
OPEN 24 HOURS

This urban park connects Market Square to Gay Street, with an ever-changing array of sculpture. It's a legacy of TVA photographer Charles Krutch, who surprised the city after his 1981 death with a major bequest to establish a previously elusive downtown park. Inscriptions honor both the benefactor, whose work has been displayed at New York's Museum of Modern Art, and his more-famous brother, author and pioneer naturalist Joseph Wood Krutch. The Krutch family, which included his uncle, landscape impressionist Charles Christopher Krutch, was known for their interest in the pre-park Smokies, and this downtown park with its faux waterfall and creek, was intended to evoke the region's wilder charms.

 ### World's Fair Park

Located at 1060 Worlds Fair Park Drive • worldsfairpark.org
EVERY DAY: 6AM–MIDNIGHT • SUNSPHERE OBSERVATION DECK: 9AM–10PM

Surely one of the region's most distinctive parks is the one where Knoxville hosted the 1982 World's Fair. Over six months, 11 million people converged on this narrow strip of urban acreage to behold dozens of international exhibits, the most popular of which was that of the People's Republic of China, marking the first time that nation had participated in a World's Fair. The site, Second Creek bottomland that had been a mostly industrial rail yard since the 19th century, now makes an interesting and sometimes surprising stroll. It combines multiple historic buildings used for the exposition (historical preservation is a rarity at world's fairs) with a few theme structures and some buildings built in the years since the fair, like the Knoxville Museum of Art, designed by nationally known museum architect Edward Larrabee Barnes and opened in 1990 (*see p.39*).

Much of the southern part of the original fair site is paved for UT parking, but the city maintains the Second Creek Greenway, an agreeable pedestrian path to UT. The South Lawn, along 11th Street, attracts Frisbee footballers, and several large events.

KRUTCH, *originally spelled* KRÜTZSCH, *is a German name, pronounced "Krootch"*

WORLD'S FAIR PARK
AMPHITHEATRE AND SUNSPHERE

The Festival Lawn includes the Court of Flags, an homage to the 23 international participants in the Fair. It attracts fountain-cavorting kids.

On or adjacent to the park are several buildings worth a glance:

At the northern end of the site is the 1871 Foundry, originally part of the Knoxville Iron Co. plant. The brick building was known as the Strohaus during the fair, a German-themed beer hall with live polka music and dancing every night; it's now a catered event space.

The prominent L&N Station and Depot, built in 1905, and described in James Agee's *A Death in the Family*, was a passenger station for 63 years. It housed restaurants during the fair, and now hosts a public STEM Academy high school. (Be careful not to approach it during the school year without permission.)

The Candy Factory, built ca. 1915, was home of Littlefield & Steere, one of the South's largest candy manufacturers. Used for multiple dining and shopping purposes during the Fair, it redeemed its original use by hosting a chocolate factory on the ground floor until 2018. For many years, the Candy Factory also housed art galleries and studios. Now it's mostly residential.

Several 1890s Victorian frame houses along the western edge of the park near Clinch hosted several different exhibits, as well as a beer garden. Today, some of them have returned to their original use as private residences.

Although most of the structures built expressly for the Fair have been demolished—including the huge U.S. Pavilion and IMAX Theatre, which were intended to be permanent—two interesting survivors include the Sunsphere and the Tennessee

THE KNOXVILLE MUSEUM OF ART

IMELDA MARCOS, *flamboyant first lady of the Philippines, visited the Fair*

Amphitheater. The former, designed by local firm Community Tectonics, is a globally unique homage to the sun, the source of all energy on Earth– an elevator ride to the inside of the lofty sphere itself will yield impressive views.

At its foot, the Tennessee Amphitheater is of special interest to students of modern architecture, as an early work of German engineer-designer Horst Berger, who later used this innovative tensile design technique in designing major international airports from Jedda to Denver.

EAST TENNESSEE VETERANS MEMORIAL

8 composers, **SERGEI RACHMANINOFF**. The 12-foot bronze is the work of Russian sculptor Viktor Bokarov, who donated his statue to Knoxville, the site of his hero's final piano performance. Rachmaninoff, seriously ill at the time of his 1943 show at UT's Alumni Hall, canceled the rest of his tour and died weeks later. Bokarov sent the statue to Knoxville because it witnessed Rachmaninoff's final performance. The surprise gift remained in storage for several years before it was bronzed and installed here in 2003.

SERGEI RACHMANINOFF STATUE IN WORLD'S FAIR PARK

In the northern part of the park, near the L&N, is the solemn marble installation the East Tennessee Veterans Memorial, with the names of more than 6,000 local soldiers who have died in wars since 1917. Its location is poignant; for hundreds who died in World War II, the L&N station formed their last glimpses of their hometown.

Also within the park, in the southwestern section, is the Western Hemisphere's only statue of one of the 20th century's great

THIS PART OF THE LAKE FROM THE WORLD'S FAIR IS NOW THE FESTIVAL LAWN INCLUDING THE POPULAR COURT OF FLAGS FOUNTAIN

The SOUTH LAWN *was the site of the* SAUDI PAVILION *and the* BUDWEISER CLYDESDALE'S STABLES

Emory Place

Located at North end of Gay Street

Downtown Knoxville's first park today offers few of the amenities of a park, but it's still a curiosity worth a visit. The odd open spot is actually a crooked cavity left by the absence of a large market building known as the Central Market, which stood here from about 1888 to 1905. During that era buildings crowded around it. When the market failed, the building was disassembled and moved to South Knoxville, and the city pounced on the opportunity to address its oft-bemoaned lack of a downtown park. Rev. Isaac Emory, a New York native who came to Tennessee at the end of the Civil War to introduce a new concept in Christian education—Sunday School—had been perhaps the best-known victim of the horrific New Market Train Wreck of 1904. Knoxville named the new park in his honor. It served as a green park, with flowers and trees and a statue, for 50 years, until the postwar demand for parking seemed to be overcoming the demand for parks. The city paved it as a parking lot. A 1987 plan by Duane Grieve, whose architecture firm was on the property, restored some of its old greenery, resulting in a plaza with both parking and green space. On certain weekend afternoons when the clientele of Crafty Bastard Brewery spills out into the open, its old park spirit returns.

EMORY PLACE TODAY

NORTH

 ## Fountain City Park

Located at 117 Hotel Avenue
EVERY DAY: DAWN-DUSK

The tree-shaded glade along a clear brook that leads from an underground stream to form First Creek is one of Knoxville's loveliest spots, perfect for strolls or picnics. Celebrated as a park as early as the 19th century, it was an agreeable spot for evangelical "camp meetings." Fountain City became a nationally advertised resort by 1885, with a hotel and golf course and the heart-shaped "lake" or duck pond.

The park itself, privately owned and informally recognized as a park, was an attraction by the 1890s, when it was the location of picnics, lectures, baseball games, "fat man races," dances, balloon ascensions, and Independence Day and Labor Day events, as well as lectures and political rallies.

EMORY PARK, 1920S

The **WALLA WALLA CHEWING GUM CO.'S FACTORY** *was once located at* **EMORY PLACE**, *ca.* 1900

Socialist Eugene V. Debs drew crowds in the thousands here in 1905. A steam-driven streetcar known as the "Dummy Line" ran regularly from downtown Knoxville.

Although the resort known as the Fountainhead Hotel closed in the early 20th century, and later burned down, the park remained popular. It became more formally declared a permanent public park in 1932 when the owner, a private utility, deeded it to the community to be run by the local Lions Club. They still maintain the park, arguably one of Knoxville's most perfect and least-changed places.

All that's left of the old hotel, besides the name "Hotel Avenue" is its heart-shaped duck pond—formally known as Fountain City Lake, one block south of the park. It's a popular fishing spot, remarkable considering its small size.

 Racheff Gardens

Located at 1943 Tennessee Avenue
MON-FRI: 9AM-3PM *closed when raining*

Little known to most Knoxvillians but astonishing in its own way, Racheff Gardens was the ca. 1950 dream of a steel-foundry executive, Bulgarian-born Ivan Racheff (1892–1982). Located at 1943 Tennessee Avenue, in Lonsdale—immediately next door to the Gerdau plant, Tennessee's only steel mill—the three-acre formal garden was intended to prove that heavy industry can be beautiful. Its aesthetic appeal is a credit to the Tennessee Federation of Garden Clubs who run it. Racheff lived in the ca. 1902 house on the property, and was known to spend his mornings enjoying the view out his second-floor window.

RACHEFF GARDENS IN LONSDALE

IVAN RACHEFF *is buried on his gardens' property*

AERIAL VIEW OF SHARP'S RIDGE, 1938

 ## Sharp's Ridge

Located at 329 Sharp's Ridge
EVERY DAY: DAWN-DUSK

This sudden steep ridge across North Knoxville separates the older parts of town from Fountain City. In military photographs of the Civil War era, Sharp's Ridge is one of the few recognizable features. Although privately owned, it was a popular hunting and camping destination by the late 19th century. After a series of private development proposals failed, the city purchased it as a memorial to soldiers of World War II, and built a road across the top of it—so steep, in spots, that some automobiles were unable to make the climb. At about the same time, as radio was booming and television was on the horizon, it began attracting proposals for establishing tall broadcast towers and even hilltop studios. Many of Knoxville's earliest TV shows, featuring live country and R&B music, and wrestling matches, with live audiences, originated on Sharp's Ridge. Formally dedicated as a war memorial in 1953, the same year its towers began broadcasting television to the region, it became an odd combination of solemn memorial and busy broadcasting center.

EAST

 ## Cal Johnson Park & Recreation Center

Located at 507 Hall of Fame Drive
RECREATION CENTER
MON-THURS: 1-9PM • FRI: 10AM-6PM

Although it looks fairly ordinary, a building big enough to hold a basketball court, alongside a few outdoor courts as well, this park's story makes it extraordinary. Established in 1922, Cal Johnson Park was named for one of its chief benefactors, an elderly philanthropist who believed in the place and spent thousands beautifying it. The extraordinary part of the story is that Cal Johnson was raised to be a slave. Through inspiration and persistence and

SHARP'S RIDGE *was briefly a* CHILDHOOD HOME *of* ADOLPH OCHS, *future publisher of the* NEW YORK TIMES

CAL JOHNSON, CA. 1920S

and '50s. Urban renewal was hard on the community, subtracting both Johnson's large marble fountain (no one knows what became of it) as well as most of its neighbors, but adding a modern athletic facility. Today the original park acreage is still there, but with more emphasis on the Rec Center than the grounds, it's mainly a place to play basketball.

some canny land deals assisted by his mother (also a former slave). Johnson built a small empire of industry and entertainment, with a clothing factory, a chain of saloons, and a horse-racing track. For almost 40 years, the park was a popular gathering place for the black community, attracting street vendors and tennis players and daydreamers, as described by poet Nikki Giovanni, who grew up just across the street in the 1940s

H ALEX HALEY HERITAGE SQUARE

Located at 1620 Dandridge Avenue
EVERY DAY: DAWN–DUSK

On the east side of downtown, adjacent to larger Morningside Park, the park sometimes known as Haley Heritage Square honors the legacy of *Roots* author Alex Haley (1921–1992), a former West Tennessean who settled in Knoxville in his later years.

 Its large bronze statue, by California sculptor Tina Allen, was the world's largest statue of an African-American at the time of its unveiling in 1996. (It's still one of the largest.) It depicts Haley reading a story, perhaps to children, who like to climb on the statue—and may, with supervision *(see p.79)*.

ALEX HALEY HERITAGE SQUARE AT MORNINGSIDE PARK

I CASWELL PARK

Located at 570 Winona Street
EVERY DAY: DAWN–DUSK

This 37-acre east-side athletic facility has deep roots. Caswell Park, on this site, was Knoxville's first big park, and became known as the city's professional baseball field. Developer William Caswell, who as a youth in the 1860s played in some of the region's first baseball games, donated the land along a big bend in First Creek in 1916. He could

WILLIAM CASWELL developed the FOURTH AND GILL neighborhood, where he lived

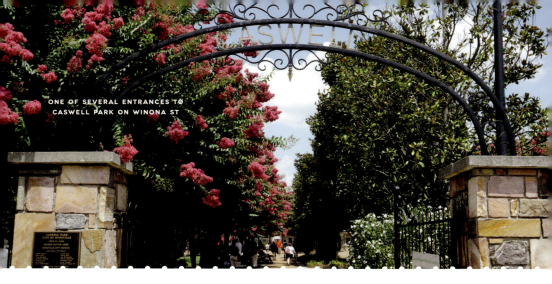

ONE OF SEVERAL ENTRANCES TO CASWELL PARK ON WINONA ST

see games from the second-floor window of his home on North Fifth Avenue. For about 80 years, Caswell Park, sometimes by other names, hosted Knoxville's minor-league baseball teams. During that time the park witnessed both major baseball stars, like the New York Yankees, starring Babe Ruth and Lou Gehrig, who played exhibition games here in the 1930s—as well as other spectacles, like Olympic star Jesse Owens' running exhibitions—and concerts, as when rock pioneer Sister Rosetta Tharp demonstrated the new electric guitar here in 1951.

It was the site of three successive baseball stadiums, the last of them Bill Meyer Stadium, built in 1953 and named for a Pittsburgh Pirates manager who was from Knoxville. Among its biggest crowds were the ones that came to see basketball legend Michael Jordan when he played several games as a Birmingham Barons outfielder here in 1994, during his brief post-basketball foray into minor-league baseball. The Knoxville Smokies left for Sevier County in 1999; Bill Meyer Stadium was torn down in 2003.

Today, most of the park is dedicated to community softball and baseball fields.

J KNOXVILLE BOTANICAL GARDEN & ARBORETUM

Located at 2743 Wimpole Avenue
865-862-8717 • knoxgarden.org
EVERY DAY: DAWN–DUSK • VISITOR CENTER MON–FRI: 9AM–4PM

Off the beaten path in the middle of East Knoxville is 47 acres of lush botanical diversity. Its history reaches back to 1786, with an orchard planted by a Revolutionary War veteran. For over two centuries, what became known as the Howell Nursery was a source for an ever-changing variety of plants, especially ornamentals. Howell became known for cultivating new strains of crepe myrtle and pink dogwood, and for interesting landscape design. As the family

BABE RUTH WITH FRIENDS AT CASWELL PARK, 1925

1940 CASWELL PARK *hosted an outdoor production of Bizet's* CARMEN

KNOXVILLE BOTANICAL GARDEN IS FULL OF LITTLE SURPRISES

relinquished the business, they contracted with local philanthropists in 2001 to create the Knoxville Botanical Garden and Arboretum. Since then, the garden has grown in interest with each new season and each imaginative innovation. Its trails present an encyclopedic array of regional flora. The Garden's growing sense of place has led some to describe the adjacent middle-class neighborhoods as "the Garden District." Note the vaguely medieval-looking round stone houses (they actually just date to the 1940s) and look for the playful memorial "Secret Garden" inspired by the novel by Frances Hodgson Burnett.

 CHILHOWEE PARK

Located at 3301 Magnolia Avenue
865-215-1450 • chilhoweepark.org
EVERY DAY: DAWN–DUSK • OFFICE HOURS MON–FRI: 8AM–4:30PM

Visitors first escaped urban stresses here in the 1880s, when Knoxville proper was starting to get crowded, noisy, and smoky. When future U.S. Treasury Secretary William Gibbs McAdoo undertook to build East Tennessee's first electric streetcar line, Chilhowee Park was a natural destination for it.

Originally known by the pun Lake Ottosee, after its large pond, it became a familiar jaunt for baseball games and holiday gatherings, often drawing thousands.

In the early 20th century, it was the venue for three huge expositions featuring orators Teddy Roosevelt, Booker T. Washington, Helen Keller, William Jennings Bryan, and others. The last such event, the National Conservation Exposition of 1913, which featured everything from motorcycle races to exhibitions of new Impressionist art, drew one million visitors.

Since 1916, it has been the home of the Tennessee Valley Fair, one of only a few of America's annual fairs that has survived into the 21st century. Featuring rides, shows, and exhibits, the fair always includes farmers' award-winning produce and farm animals.

For years, Chilhowee Park featured a small amusement park, which during the Jim Crow era was whites only except for Aug. 8, celebrated in East Tennessee as Emancipation Day. However, blacks often attended shows in the Chilhowee Park auditorium. The Jacob Building, built in 1941 to replace a previous, grander exhibition building destroyed in a 1938 fire, is used for presentations and exhibits today, but in the 1940s and '50s, it hosted an extraordinary series of jazz and R&B performers, including Duke Ellington, Louis Armstrong, Tommy Dorsey, and Lionel Hampton—as well as rock 'n' roll pioneers Fats Domino, Chuck Berry, Little Richard, Big Mama Thornton, Ike and Tina Turner, Bo Diddley, and the young James Brown.

TENNESSEE VALLEY FAIR, A PERENNIAL FALL TRADITION, SEEN HERE IN 1937

A JAMES AGEE *story describes his* FATHER'S FIGHT *with a Chilhowee Park* CARNY, *ca.* 1915

CHILHOWEE PARK'S RESTORED 1910 MARBLE BANDSTAND

The annual fair was the subject of the first publication by Cormac McCarthy; in 1950, the Catholic High student wrote a drily humorous confession about sneaking into the fair. Three years later, in 1953, two other local high-school students, Don and Phil Everly, were here at the fair when they first met guitar wizard Chet Atkins, who became their mentor and producer.

Chilhowee Park once resembled a small city of white buildings built for the Edwardian-era expositions, but one by one, they were all removed or burned. And today, "Lake Ottosee," no longer called that, is much smaller than it was. All that remains of that era is the one marble gazebo on a hilltop, built in 1910 and used as a bandstand during the exposition era.

 Zoo Knoxville

Located at 3500 Knoxville Zoo Drive 865-637-5331 • zooknoxville.org
EVERY DAY: 10AM–4PM
Last admission 1 hr before closing

Knoxville's respected zoological park originated as a small "Birthday Park" for poor children in 1935. After some years of neglect and abuse, it was reborn as a makeshift zoo in 1948, featuring mainly exotic former pets—like an overgrown alligator—and odd animals the police had collared on their rounds. It became the Municipal Zoo in 1951, and after some economic and management challenges, was reborn as the Knoxville Zoo in 1972. Its modern incarnation boasts several distinctions. It hosted the first African elephant born in the Western Hemisphere in 1978, and continues its rare program for red pandas.

 Holston River Park

Located at 3300 Holston Hills Road
EVERY DAY: DAWN–DUSK

Although a relatively recent park (ca. 1994), it highlights a lovely portion of the Holston River, which flows from Virginia, before its junction with the French Broad to form the Tennessee. From here you can see, up close, Boyd's Island, once farmed, and occasionally, in the earliest days of aviation, a landing field.

HORSE STUNTS AT THE 1910 APPALACHIAN EXPOSITION AT CHILHOWEE PARK

Star animal handler **JACK HANNA** *worked at the* **KNOXVILLE ZOO** *in the early '70s*

HIGH GROUND PARK AROUND THE RUINS OF 1863 UNION FORT HIGLEY

PARKS & GARDENS

SOUTH

 10 *Fort Dickerson Park*

Located at 3000 Fort Dickerson Road
EVERY DAY: DAWN–DUSK
SEE CIVIL WAR P.94

Almost forgotten for decades, Fort Dickerson was "discovered" in 1935, when city officials encountered its ruins within a remote, wooded hilltop jungle. What remains visible here was built by occupying Union troops in the fall of 1863, when it was critical to the Union defense to hold these heights from which enemy cannons could seriously damage the city. Though never assaulted, Fort Dickerson traded artillery fire with an advance guard of Confederates during the siege of Knoxville. Supplied with a road, it has been a public park since 1957. It drew thousands in 1963 when it was the site of a noisy centennial re-enactment. It has recently been the subject of a major improvement financed by the Aslan Foundation.

 11 *High Ground Park / Fort Higley*

Located at 1000 Cherokee Trail
EVERY DAY: DAWN–DUSK
SEE CIVIL WAR P.95

For decades, the earthworks off Cherokee Trail were known to only the most intrepid Civil War buffs willing to thrash through the underbrush to behold it. It became better known to the public at large in the early 21st century when it was threatened with a major condo development project.

The charitable Aslan Foundation purchased the property and established High Ground Park on Cherokee Trail, completed just in time for the sesquicentennial of the siege of Knoxville in 2013. Now with parking and easy paths, it offers abundant interpretive signage about the campaign and the more furtive battles on the south side of the river. The Union "redan," or small fortified cannon emplacement, is no bigger than a boxing ring, but a rarity. Long sought by trespassing hikers, it's now easier and safer to see.

The southside HILLTOP FORT RUINS *may someday be linked by* TRAILS

153

MEAD'S QUARRY, 1920S

 I<small>JAMS</small> N<small>ATURE</small> C<small>ENTER</small>

Located at 2915 Island Home Avenue
865-577-4717 • *ijams.org*
EVERY DAY: 8AM–DUSK
VISTOR CENTER MON–SAT: 9AM–5PM
SUN: 11AM–5PM

Originally it was just a semi-private riverside bird sanctuary with an almost Edwardian languor, home to illustrator/ornithologist Harry Ijams (1876–1954) and his family in which daughters outnumbered adults. For decades after Ijams' death, it remained a quiet retreat for garden clubs. However, in the early 21st century, through a combination of philanthropy, hard work, and serendipity, Ijams acquired hundreds of acres of adjacent quarry property.

Today, Ijams, an active place for hiking, mountain biking, rock climbing, boating, and treetops ropes-course challenges, still maintains its central mission of environmental education espoused by the Ijams family. The visitor center houses non-releasable wildlife and several exhibits including an extremely rare pair of mounted ivory-billed woodpeckers, given to Ijams by a Catholic priest in memory of ornithologist James T. Tanner, who with his wife Nancy witnessed the last confirmed wild sightings of the bird in Louisiana in the 1940s. Ijams retains a strong birding focus and includes several bird-themed interpretive trails.

The Ijams home is gone, but the basic layout of the original sanctuary is intact. The 300+ acre property includes several protected caves. The one along the wooden river boardwalk was a favorite canoeing destination from downtown in the Victorian era—and later became known as Maude Moore's Cave. In 1919 it served as a hideout for its honoree who had killed a man in Knoxville in self-defense.

Divided by Island Home Avenue, Mead's and Ross Marble Quarries are now listed on the National Register of Historic Places. From here Tennessee pink marble made its way to national buildings and monuments, notably the J.P. Morgan Library in New York and the

IJAMS FAMILY HOME, LATE 1920S

Often mispronounced, I<small>JAMS</small> *rhymes with* "R<small>HYMES</small>." *The* J *is silent.*

National Gallery of Art in Washington, D.C. Old quarries tell the story of an old industry, but they left some extraordinary topography, creating fantastic micro-landscapes of cliffs and ravines, gradually being reclaimed by nature. Look for the site's most unusual feature, a man-made rock bridge known as the "Keyhole" (*see p.18*).

THE OLD CITY INTAKE PLANT, A RUIN OF WHICH STILL EXISTS, VISIBLE FROM SUTTREE LANDING

SUTTREE LANDING PARK

Located at 1001 Waterfront Drive
EVERY DAY: DAWN–DUSK

A relatively new city park got its unusual name as a result of an Internet poll. Author Cormac McCarthy's 1979 novel *Suttree*, set in 1951, concerns a disaffected fisherman who spends much of his time along these banks. Only after the park's completion in 2016 did historians discover that the same riverside plot had been used as early as 1880 as a horse-racing track. Its half-mile oval also hosted bicycle races, droll "jousting tournaments," and some of the university's first track meets. There's no trace of the oval today, but the park features long riverside walkways and picnic tables. From here you can see, across the river, a peculiar stone pillbox-like structure, with apertures—it's not a fort, but the ca. 1890 intake structure for the city's first water-treatment plant. It has not been used for that purpose since the 1920s, but still makes an eye-catching landmark.

MARY VESTAL PARK

Located at 401 Maryville Pike
EVERY DAY: DAWN–DUSK

Named for the mother of two brothers who established the Vestal Lumber Co., Mary Vestal Park has been a South Knoxville refuge since 1949, when it hosted baseball games, a playground, and sometimes open-air theater. Originally just nine acres, it has doubled in size.

SUTTREE LANDING PARK

1880s | *The* **RIVERSIDE RACE TRACK** *hosted black and white bicycle races*

WEST

Q James Agee Park

Located at 331 James Agee Street
EVERY DAY: DAWN–DUSK

This one-lot pocket park honors the memory of author James Agee, who was born in this neighborhood, lived less than a block to the north, and evoked his Highland Avenue home for the setting of a couple of his most famous works, *A Death in the Family* and "Knoxville: Summer 1915." Spearheaded by poet and songwriter R.B. Morris, with support from several others, including novelist Wilma Dykeman (1920–2006), it was completed as a rare joint effort between the city and the university. Agee's daughter, DeeDee, was on hand for its 2003 dedication.

FORT SANDERS' JAMES AGEE PARK ON JAMES AGEE ST

7 Circle Park

Located at Circle Park Drive
SEE UNIVERSITY OF TENNESSEE P.105

On first glance, it might seem like modern landscaping from UT's rapid expansions in the latter half of the 20th century—but Circle Park was actually a public park decades before it was associated with the university. It has been claimed to be Knoxville's first public park, known as "the Circle" by 1886. Some of its features are unusual, like the exposed limestone, and it's one of the two likeliest contenders for the still-unknown park project on which internationally famous landscape architect Frederick Law Olmsted was working when he spent time in Knoxville in 1893. Although it was there in some form before Olmsted's mysterious effort, it bears a few hallmarks of Olmsted's style.

Once ringed with Victorian mansions, Circle Park was popular, and became the destination of an electric streetcar line from downtown. UT took it over by degrees in the 1960s, as the university acquired each of the large houses on Circle Park's perimeter and replaced them with modern academic buildings. But the park, unlike anything else in his neighborhood, has survived in a form that Victorians would recognize.

R Lakeshore Park

Located at 6410 South Northshore Dr
865-215-1722 • lakeshorepark knoxville.org • EVERY DAY: DAWN–10PM

One of Knoxville's most popular parks has an especially unusual history. For more than a century, this was the campus of East Tennessee's main public mental institution.

A CENTENNIAL COMMEMORATION *of Agee's famous piece drew a* CAPACITY CROWD *to the park*

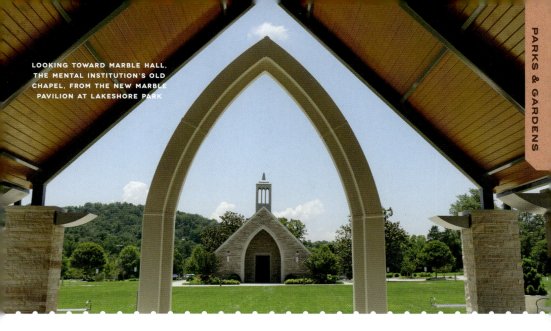

LOOKING TOWARD MARBLE HALL, THE MENTAL INSTITUTION'S OLD CHAPEL, FROM THE NEW MARBLE PAVILION AT LAKESHORE PARK

PARKS & GARDENS

Finished in 1886, the state facility was often called the Lyons View Asylum, in its early years, and was the Bearden area's major employer. One of several original castle-like buildings remains at the top of the hill.

The campus included its own power plant, and more than 20 buildings, including dormitories. For years, as many as 3,000 mental patients lived here. Some spent their lives here, working on the farm—it was almost self-sustaining—and attending dances, movies, and other special events, including concerts. (Perhaps the biggest one ever was in early 1972, when Johnny Cash, June Carter, Carl Perkins and others performed for the patients here.)

It has an unexpected literary heritage. In Tennessee Williams' play *Suddenly Last Summer*, a Louisiana mental institution is called "Lion's View"; the playwright's father was from Knoxville, and Williams, a frequent visitor in his youth, obviously associated the phrase with the old "Lyons View Asylum." Sometimes known as Eastern State, this actual facility appears as a setting in Cormac McCarthy's novel, *Child of God*, and Peter Taylor's novel, *In the Tennessee Country*.

The campus was off limits for Knoxvillians for decades, but in the 1980s, as the institution downscaled, mainstreaming most of its patients, the city began using parts of it. Lakeshore Park was formally established in 1993, and coexisted with continuing operations of the mental-health facilities, for almost 20 years. Lakeshore Mental Health Institute finally closed in 2012, and most of its remaining buildings were torn down. Besides the original administration building on the hilltop, the park retains the 1960 chapel (Marble Hall), admired for its modernist design.

THE FORMER "EASTERN HOSPITAL FOR THE INSANE," NOW LAKESHORE PARK

MARCUS DELAFAYETTE BEARDEN *died before the 1886 completion of the institution he enabled*

Sequoyah Hills Park

Located along Cherokee Boulevard
EVERY DAY: DAWN–DUSK

This long river park existed before it was improved by TVA, which by the early 1940s had made it less prone to flooding. It follows the perimeter of old Looney's Bend, the term riverboatmen still use to refer to this peninsula. An Indian mound of apparently debatable age and purpose, judging by the conflicting signage on either side of the mound, overlooks the easternmost boat-ramp parking area.

The baseball fields here date back to the 1920s, and were once known as the Polo Field, though stories of actual polo games ever being played there are vague.

 ## Tyson Park

Located at 2351 Kingston Pike
EVERY DAY: DAWN–DUSK

Dating to 1929, Tyson Park was arguably the city's first large modern park, with multiple facilities. Enabled by Bettie Tyson, it honors her son, McGhee Tyson, killed in World War I, for whom the airport is also named. The Tysons' gift of the park to the city is connected to a contingency: that the city's airport be always named for their son.

The acreage actually has a prehistory, though—by 1898, it was private property, owned by the Tysons, who apparently tolerated a local group's nine-hole golf course, probably the first approximation of a golf course in Knoxville. Among golfers, the creek was known ominously as "the Styx." The golf course disappeared a century ago, but Tyson hosts multiple tennis courts, picnic tables and barbecue grills, playground equipment, and, in recent years, the city's only public skateboard park.

 ## Third Creek Greenway

Entrances at 3507 & 2321 Kingston Pike, 3110 Sutherland Avenue & 104 North Forest Park Boulevard
OPEN 24 HOURS

After eight years of failed attempts to connect Knoxville to the Smokies with an extensive bike trail, Knoxville's first greenway, a two-mile route along Third Creek west of Tyson Park, was completed in 1974. For 15 years,

MCGHEE TYSON AIRPORT, 1939

Many of Knoxville's BEST PARKS *are along* RIVER *and* CREEK FLOODPLAINS

RAILROAD TRESTLE AT THE THIRD CREEK GREENWAY TRAIL

PARKS & GARDENS

HOLOCAUST MEMORIAL STONE AT WEST HILLS PARK

it was the only bike trail in town. But by the 1990s, it had connected to the river at the mouth of Third Creek, and a miles-long new bike trail by the river to Volunteer Landing and points east. Now it stretches much farther west into Bearden. Accessible by foot or bicycle, points of interest along the trail include Highland Memorial Cemetery (see p.172); Everly Brothers Park, not far from where the famous duo lived when they began experimenting with rock 'n' roll; West High,

where they attended school—which is also the site of the original McGhee Tyson Airport, ca. 1929–1937; the presumed Civil War fort ruin at the trestle (see p.97); Tyson Park (see p.158); Fulton Bottoms Field, venerable soccer and rugby field originally alongside the long-gone ca. 1915 Fulton Bellows plant; and UT Ag Campus and gardens (see p.112).

West Hills / John Bynon Park

Located at 410 North Winston Road
EVERY DAY: DAWN–DUSK

A few steps off the walking and biking trail from the North Winston Road entrance, just half a mile off Kingston Pike, stands an interesting international memorial for the victims of the Holocaust during World War II. An inscribed rock, surrounded by semi-circles of trees and stacked stones was dedicated in 2005 on Holocaust Remembrance Day. That day, held each spring, honors victims, survivors, and those servicemen who liberated the survivors from the Nazi death camps.

A BICYCLIST *can ride from* DOWNTOWN *to* BEARDEN *crossing only* THREE STREETS

UNION MONUMENT, NATIONAL CEMETERY

CEMETERIES

Knoxville is home to hundreds of cemeteries, churchyards, and old family graveyards. Many graves are too worn to read, but the oldest legible gravestone dates to 1793—that of Samuel Carrick's wife, Elizabeth, at Lebanon at the Forks Cemetery.

Knoxville offers a virtual history of the American cemetery, from the churchyards and family plots known to the early settlers, to the stylish Garden Cemeteries of the mid-19th century, to the formal military cemeteries that started with the Civil War. Most are safe and well-kept. A few are obscure and overgrown. Listed here are just a few of the most historic and easiest to visit.

Note: Please remember that, except for military cemeteries, most of Knoxville's graveyards are private property, and governed either by the business that runs the cemetery, a church, or a foundation. Although polite visitors are usually welcome in the daytime, some cemeteries prefer that you seek permission from the main office.

DOWNTOWN

 ### First Presbyterian

Located at 620 State Street

First Presbyterian churchyard's downtown space was a gift of settler James White, whose original 1786 fort was immediately north of this site. He surrendered his turnip patch for the establishment of a church and cemetery; the city had immediate use for a cemetery, and it was established about 20 years before the 1816 construction of the church. White and his family are buried here. Knoxville's oldest graveyard was here in the 1790s, when visitors remarked on it, though the oldest grave legible today dates to 1800. That one happens to be among the churchyard's most famous. It's the horizontal stone belonging to William Blount, signer of the U.S. Constitution (the only one buried outside of the original 13 colonies); the first and only governor of the Southwestern Territory; and, albeit briefly, one of Tennessee's first two U.S. senators. His wife Mary, namesake of both Maryville and Grainger County, is buried at his side.

GRAVESTONE OF SAMUEL CARRICK (1760-1809) FOUNDER OF KNOXVILLE'S FIRST CHURCH

1799 MORAVIAN MISSIONARIES *described First Presbyterian's* GRAVEYARD

MARGUERITE DABNEY'S MONUMENT, FIRST PRESBYTERIANS ONLY CROSS

Others buried here include U.S senators John Williams (an ancestor of the playwright Tennessee Williams), and Hugh Lawson White. Both became opponents of the first Tennessee president, Andrew Jackson. White, who was for a few months president pro tempore of the U.S. Senate, ran for president in 1836, an anti-Jacksonian gesture that helped spawn the Whig Party. Other notables include Samuel Carrick, founder of Knoxville's first church, First Presbyterian—and also founder of Blount College, which evolved into the University of Tennessee.

According to an early description, the graveyard is the resting place of people "of all races and creeds." The graveyard was closed to new burials in the 1850s, as cemeteries were moving to larger fields in rural areas.

Note the scarcity of religious icons, like crosses. The graveyard includes only one crucifix, a Celtic cross near the front, a later memorial to a teenaged girl, Marguerite Dabney, who's buried elsewhere. That lack of crosses reflects the early Protestants' skepticism of graven images. Crucifixes were not seen widely in this part of the country until after the Civil War.

Also of interest are a particular concentration of death dates. About one tenth of all the graves in this churchyard date to the summer and fall of 1838, the era of perhaps the worst epidemic in Knoxville history—"the fever that was fatal to so many," as one stone's inscription describes it. Its cause remains unknown.

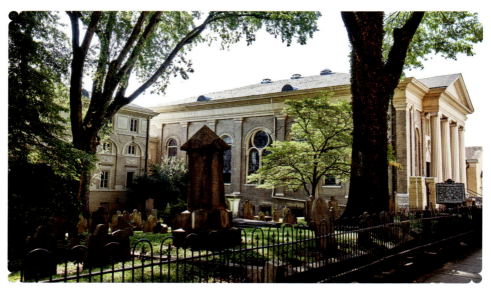

FIRST PRESBYTERIAN GRAVEYARD ON STATE ST

The oldest graveyard welcomes a noisy **EGG HUNT** *each* **EASTER SUNDAY**

OLD GRAY, WITH ITS PARK-LIKE SETTING, IS JUST A SHORT WALK FROM DOWNTOWN

 Old Gray

Located at 543 North Broadway
865-522-1424 • oldgraycemetery.org

Across 14 acres of wooded hills, Old Gray Cemetery makes for a fascinating afternoon walk, and probably has more history per minute of strolling than any other cemetery in the region. Founded in 1850, its name has nothing to do with the Civil War—a common misperception—or with the color of its stones. It's in honor of Thomas Gray, the English poet famous for "Elegy Written in a Country Churchyard." Within walking distance of downtown (near the far northern end of Gay Street, in fact), Old Gray is Knoxville's best example of the "Garden Cemetery" movement that began in Paris in the early 19th century, which pictured cemeteries as lovely parks to be visited, with horticulture and meandering lanes. Although privately owned, from its earliest days Old Gray stood in for a public park in a city that lacked one.

STATUE MEMORIALIZES LILLIEN GAINES WHO DIED AT AGE 7 IN 1876

Most of **OLD GRAY'S STATUES** *depict girls and women who died young*

Old Gray reflects both sides of the Civil War—the fiery Unionist "Parson" W.G. Brownlow is prominently buried here, as is Rep. Horace Maynard, a Lincoln ally who kept his seat in U.S. Congress even after his state had gone Confederate. And there are lots of Confederates here, including Col. Henry Ashby, shot to death in a partisan fight in 1868, and memorialized near Brownlow. But more than anything, Old Gray reflects Knoxville's burgeoning growth as a city in the late 19th and early 20th centuries, with connections to American and even world history.

Old-family Knoxvillians like the McClungs and the Williamses (including playwright Tennessee Williams' father and grandparents), mixed with immigrants from Germany, Switzerland, Ireland, France, Italy, and Greece. (Two stones here, in fact, are carved entirely in Greek.) Although the overwhelming majority of those buried here are white, each plot owner decided whom to include, and Old Gray is a resting place of at least six black people, including some former slaves.

OLD GRAY LOOKING NORTH TO NATIONAL CEMETERY

Graves of interest include those of ambassador-scholar Ebenezer Alexander, who was involved in founding the modern Olympic Games in Athens in 1896; Gen. Lawrence Davis Tyson, and his son, McGhee Tyson, for whom the airport is named; influential suffragist Lizzie Crozier French; Lee McClung, who became U.S. Treasurer only after he became one of America's first national football stars, playing for Yale in the 1880s; Eliza Hodgson, mother of novelist Frances Hodgson Burnett; Gustavus Knabe, the Leipzig-born Mendelssohn associate who brought classical music to the region; impressionist artist Catherine Wiley; and all three victims of the notorious Mabry-O'Conner gunfight of Oct. 19, 1882 *(see p.32)*.

 ## National Cemetery

Located at 939 Tyson St

Knoxville National Cemetery is adjacent to Old Gray, but could hardly be more different in appearance. Flatter, sunnier, and with its mostly uniform white stones within an unusual concentric-circle plan, it

TENNESSEE WILLIAMS' GRANDMOTHER, BELLE COFFIN WILLIAMS (1853-1884)

Before Knoxville had PUBLIC PARKS, *families would* PICNIC *at* OLD GRAY

"GRAVES OF THE HIGHLANDERS, SOLDIERS CEMETERY KNOXVILLE, TENN." CA. 1864

looks modern. However, it was established only 13 years after Old Gray, as a necessity of war. Originally it was intended for Union soldiers who died in East Tennessee and other mid-South battles but couldn't be sent home for family burial. Over 3,000 of these graves are Civil War graves, and a third of those are "Unknowns." Among them are many "colored troops," identified by the abbreviation CLD, who were involved in the Union occupation of Knoxville, 1863–1866.

Union veterans commenced planning a monument in the 1890s. It's had a dramatic story in itself. The first monument, constructed after years of delay in 1901, featured a large bronze eagle on its top, its wings spread as if ready to swoop. It was struck by lightning during a summer storm in 1904, and destroyed, damaging the castle-like structure beneath it. The current monument, with a dispassionate soldier's statute on top, is all stone. Completed in 1906, it has never drawn lightning.

What had been a Civil War graveyard was opened to new U.S. burials during the Spanish-American War of 1898, and then again during World War I. It has been the burial place of soldiers in every major conflict since. It includes the graves of World War II Medal of Honor winner Troy McGill, who died alone fighting Japanese in hand-to-hand combat. And for those who recognize the name as one of the winningest college-football coaches in history—and as the honoree of the enormous stadium on UT's campus—the single most startling grave here may be that of Gen. Robert Neyland, veteran of both world wars, who despite his fame, wanted a simple soldier's stone and a burial among his comrades in arms.

Knoxville has also two East Tennessee State Veterans Cemeteries, both established in relatively recent years—one at 5901 Lyons View Pike, and one near the French Broad River at 2200 East Governor John Sevier Highway.

1863 | Establishing a UNION CEMETERY was a PRIORITY for GEN. BURNSIDE, upon his arrival

ANCIENT ADAIR OAK, LYNNHURST CEMETERY

NORTH

 Lynnhurst Cemetery

Located at 2300 West Adair Drive

Fountain City's Lynnhurst (also known as Berry Lynnhurst) is a 130-acre memorial park distinguished for some historic burials but also for its Adair Oak, an enormous tree believed to date to 1777, before there were permanent white settlers in the area. Those buried here include former Pittsburgh Pirates manager Billy Meyer (1892–1957; Knoxville's old ball park was named for him)—and, a bit of a surprise—James Pope (1884–1966), former mayor of Boise and U.S. senator from Idaho. He moved to Knoxville in 1939 to take a position as a director of TVA, and stayed.

 Greenwood Cemetery

Located at 3500 Old Tazewell Pike

From Tazewell Pike, in northeast Knoxville, near Fountain City, Greenwood Cemetery looks like any modern cemetery, with mostly simple stones in mown grass, but it's older than it looks, and holds a great deal of history. Its founder was successful dentist Reuben N. Kesterson, motivated to memorialize a son who died at age 12 in 1890. Since then it has become the resting place of Knoxville's only U.S. Supreme Court justice, Edward Terry Sanford; Lowell Blanchard, radio host and country-music impresario who helped launch the careers of Chet Atkins and many others; African-American artist Joseph Delaney, known for his New York street scenes; World War I Medal of Honor winner J.E. "Buck"

KESTERSON MONUMENT AT GREENWOOD CEMETERY, PERHAPS KNOXVILLE'S TALLEST GRAVE

The iconic BUTTERFLY SCENE *in Agee's* A DEATH IN THE FAMILY *takes place at* GREENWOOD

Karnes; architects George Barber and his son, Charles; and Ellen McClung Berry, the heiress whose gothically tragic long life became the subject of a book. Also here is George Dempster, Knoxville civic leader who also happened to invent an ingenious device he named for himself, sort of: the Dumpster. Greenwood is the site of what may be region's tallest marble obelisk, the Kesterson memorial, where the cemetery's founders are buried. But lovers of literature know Greenwood for the fact that it presents one of the final scenes in the Pulitzer Prizewinning novel, *A Death in the Family*. James Agee's father—"Jay" in the novel, his name was also James—was buried here after his death in a car wreck in 1916.

EAST

CALVARY CEMETERY

Located at 1926 Martin Luther King

Calvary is Knoxville's historic Catholic Cemetery, established soon after waves of immigration from Germany and especially Ireland in the mid-19th century landed hundreds of Roman Catholics in this part of the country. Here are the graves of several early cultural leaders, like Irish-born saloonkeeper Patrick Sullivan and Knoxville Mayors John T. O'Connor and John P. Murphy (who enjoyed a longer career as the honorary "Mayor of Irish Town"). It was likely Knoxville's first cemetery to feature crucifixes and statuary, never a part of antebellum protestant cemeteries. Another unusual distinction is the array of monuments marking the 14 Stations of the Cross, spaced apart from each other in a circular walk, for those who observe that ancient Lenten tradition.

BETHEL CEMETERY

Located at 1917 Bethel Avenue

Bethel Cemetery, also known as Confederate Cemetery, is adjacent to Calvary, immediately to the southeast. It's private, but open mid-day Saturdays and by appointment with the staff of Mabry Hazen House. Most of its graves are those of more than 1,600 enlisted men who didn't have the resources to be buried elsewhere; their graves are unmarked except for a tall statue of a Confederate soldier erected 27 years after the war.

The first monument to the Civil War, that lofty statue has been described as bold, even "audacious." It's designer was artist Lloyd Branson, an apparent non-partisan who was also noted for a heroic portrait of Union Admiral Farragut. This statue stirred interest in establishing Union monuments elsewhere in town. The enclosure actually includes some non-Confederates, including about 50 Union soldiers who died in custody, as well as several civilians.

CALVARY CEMETERY

Many of those buried at **CALVARY CEMETERY** *once lived in Knoxville's* **IRISH TOWN**

Potters Field Cemetery

Located at Kyle Street near Martin Luther King Jr. Boulevard

Also known as the County Cemetery, Potters Field is across the street from Odd Fellows, and was from the mid-19th century up until about 1940 where Knoxville buried its homeless and unknowns. Records are imperfect, and most of its graves are unmarked, but there are reportedly tens of thousands of people buried here under a single melancholy monument erected toward the end of its use.

 ## Odd Fellows Cemetery

Located at 2001 Bethel Avenue

Odd Fellows is Knoxville's best-known African-American cemetery, established in 1880 by the popular 19th-century fraternal organization of that name. Though founded well after emancipation, it's believed to hold the graves of several hundred former slaves. Among its inhabitants is Cal Johnson (1844–1925) whose astonishing career in business and real estate took him from

ODD FELLOWS CEMETERY

CAL JOHNSON GRAVE AT ODD FELLOWS CEMETERY

slavery to wealth and even philanthropy; William Yardley, longtime Knoxville attorney and publisher who, after he was elected to Knoxville's Board of Aldermen, ran for governor in 1876; and Rev. Samuel and Delia Delaney, whose sons Beauford and Joseph both became nationally known artists in the wake of the Harlem Renaissance.

 ## Old Jewish Cemetery

Located at 1506 Linden Avenue

Also known as Hebrew Benevolent Society Cemetery, this tiny and little known cemetery is located in an otherwise light industrial area near Winona Street. Established mainly by and for European immigrants around the time of the Civil War, it includes some graves carved entirely in Hebrew. The story goes that the first Jewish religious organization was founded by the emergency of burial of a Jewish Confederate soldier here on ground sanctified according to Jewish custom for the purpose. Although small, it appears the graveyard was never completely filled before the establishment of another, much larger cemetery, today known as New Jewish Cemetery on Glenn Avenue (*see p.171*).

Recent **EMANCIPATION DAY** *ceremonies have highlighted* **SLAVE GRAVES** *at* **ODD FELLOWS**

RAMSEY FAMILY GRAVES AT
LEBANON-IN-THE-FORKS CEMETERY

LEBANON-IN-THE-FORKS CEMETERY

 LEBANON-IN-THE-FORKS CEMETERY

Located at 2390 Asbury Road

Knox County's first graveyard, still outside of city limits, is a little older than any graveyard in town. Formerly a churchyard for a long-gone Presbyterian church, it includes the 1793 grave of Elizabeth Carrick. Wife of founding Presbyterian minister and university forefather Samuel Carrick, she died during a terrifying moment when Knoxville was under threat of a major Chickamaugan Indian attack. Since her husband and the settlement's other men were away in the elaborate defense of town, she was buried entirely by women. Also buried here is J.G.M. Ramsey, the physician who lived near here and was one of Tennessee's first historians.

Near Lebanon in the Forks cemetery lies **ASBURY CEMETERY** at 5100 Asbury Cemetery Road which includes the remarkable grave of A.J. "Pete" Kreis, the early automobile racer whose death at the Indianapolis Speedway in 1934 is graphically depicted by sculptor Albert Milani.

A.J. "PETE" KREIS MEMORIAL, DESIGNED BY ALBERT MILANI, FEATURES THE "INDY" TRACK AND HIS RACECAR CARVED IN MARBLE AT THE POINT IT LEFT THE TRACK DURING HIS FATAL WRECK IN 1934

1828 | *The* FIRST STEAM RIVERBOAT *seen in the region made landfall near here*

SOUTH

 WOODLAWN CEMETERY

Located at 4500 Woodlawn Pike

Woodlawn is South Knoxville's largest historic cemetery, and though less well known than some of the others, makes for a lovely walk among trees and rolling hills. It's the resting place of millionaire grocer-impresario Cas Walker (1903–1998), who helped launch the careers of Dolly Parton and others; Ken Burkhart (1915–2004), who pitched for the Cardinals and the Reds in the 1940s, before an injury inspired a longer career as a Major League umpire; and Robert Saylor, one of two Knoxville policemen badly wounded in a saloon fight with Wild West outlaw Harvey Logan in 1901.

SULTANA MONUMENT, MT. OLIVE CEMETERY

 ISLAND HOME BAPTIST CHURCH at 2323 Island Home Avenue holds the unusually large and stylish 1938 grave of Pulitzer-winning reporter Paul Y. Anderson, purchased by his national friends and colleagues.

 MOUNT OLIVE CEMETERY

Located at 2420 Maryville Pike

The cemetery includes an extraordinary memorial to America's deadliest naval catastrophe, the explosion of the Sultana in the Mississippi River in April, 1865, killing well over 1,000 men, most of them Union soldiers recently released from Confederate prison camps. The loss was felt acutely in Knoxville, because hundreds of the victims were on their way home back to East Tennessee. The large stone includes a bas relief depicting the Sultana and a list of almost 400 names of Tennesseans who were aboard the ill-fated ship that night.

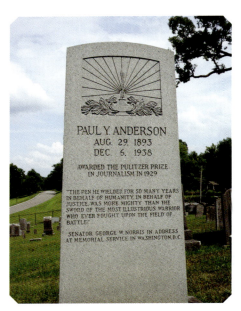

PAUL Y. ANDERSON GRAVE, ISLAND HOME BAPTIST CHURCH

National columnist **HEYWOOD BROUN** *led the effort to* **MEMORIALIZE ANDERSON**; *he died one year later*

WEST

P New Jewish Cemetery

Located at 1800 Glenn Avenue

Founded in the 19th century and still active today, New Jewish Cemetery is in the West View area. Pebbles placed on gravestones, by the old Jewish custom, prove that it's frequently visited. Among its memorialized is Harold Shersky, beloved restaurateur who ran a kosher-style deli downtown for 57 years; Louis Lippner, the Viennese fishmonger who was the most durable merchant in Market Square history, there daily for more than 60 years; Isaac Winick, the Russian immigrant who was an influential early orthodox rabbi; and Max Friedman, Ukrainian immigrant and longtime City Councilman who sometimes served as a Democratic Party adviser on a national stage. Included is a notable 1948 marble monument to the "Valiant Sons of Israel" who died in World War II.

NEW JEWISH CEMETERY ON GLENN AVE

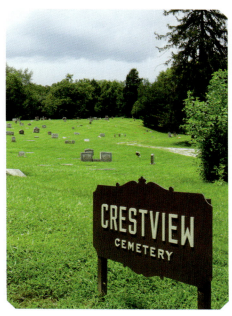

CRESTVIEW IS JUST ONE OF SEVERAL CEMETERIES ALONG KEITH AVE IN WESTVIEW

Q West View Cemeteries

Located along Keith Avenue

Along Keith Avenue are three cemeteries established in the late 19th century, northwest of downtown and just over the ridge from New Gray, but intended for blacks: Crestview, Longview, and Southern Chain. Although once a prestigious place for burials, by the late 20th century they were suffering from long-term maintenance issues, with much of this hillside thickly overgrown. Some families who could afford to exhume their loved ones had them buried them elsewhere. In recent years, community efforts have gone a long way in cleaning it up and making it easier to visit. Among those buried is Charles W. Cansler (1871–1953), a noted author, educator, and civil-rights advocate. The hilltop offers surprising views.

The **KEITH AVENUE CEMETERIES** *are just over the ridge from* **NEW GRAY**

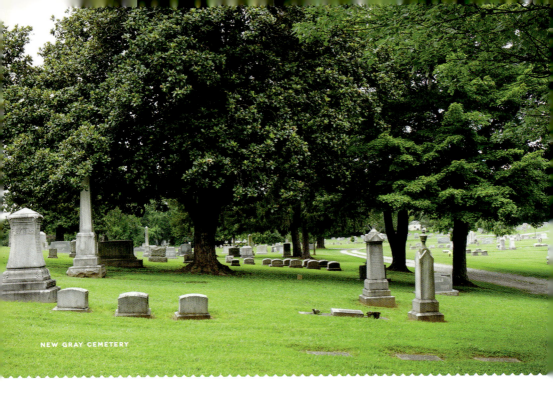

NEW GRAY CEMETERY

 R **NEW GRAY**

Located at 2724 Western Avenue

Although founded in 1892, that's still "new," compared to its namesake. Much larger and almost two miles west of Old Gray, with which it's not otherwise associated, New Gray looks modern from the street, but contains several elaborate Victorian stones, and among those interred here are veterans of both sides of the Civil War.

BLUES SINGER, IDA COX, 1930S

Members of many of Knoxville's leading families are buried here, but its most nationally famous occupant may be 1920s and '30s jazz and blues singer Ida Cox, who wrote "Wild Women Don't Have the Blues." Zaevion Dobson, the high-school student who stirred national attention when he died protecting his friends from a drive-by shooting in 2015, is also buried here.

 S **HIGHLAND MEMORIAL**

Located at 4401 Sutherland Avenue

Established in the late 19th century, Bearden's largest cemetery scales a ridge between Kingston Pike and I-40. Also known as Berry

NEW GRAY *was in the* QUIET COUNTRYSIDE *when it was established in the* 1890s

Highland, it contains the graves of industrial inventor Weston Fulton (the especially graceful neoclassical grave, established after his teenage son's death in a 1929 car wreck, was visible from the Fulton mansion on Lyons View, half a mile away); UT basketball coach Ray Mears (1926–2007) who, as his inscription makes very clear, coined the phrase "Big Orange Country"; U.S. Sen. John Knight Shields (1858–1934); commercial artist and naturalist Harry Ijams (1876–1954), whose family plot is marked by a striking chunk of granite; Medal of Honor recipient Alexander Bonnyman, Jr. (1910–1943), who died in combat with the Japanese; and World War II ace fighter pilot Bruce Holloway (1912–1999), who became a four-star general in the U.S. Air Force.

Bearden's namesake, civic leader and politician Marcus DeLafayette Bearden (the younger), was buried in a rural family plot in 1885, before this cemetery was established, but his family memorialized him here with a marker *(see p.136)*.

IJAMS FAMILY GRAVE, HIGHLAND CEMETERY

Also worthy of mention on the west side:

Dowell Springs Historic Setting is part of a recent commercial development alongside the 1858 Lonas-Dowell House, and includes a reputed slave cemetery.

Pleasant Valley Cemetery at 401 Concord Road in Farragut includes the grave of Archibald Roane (1759–1819), second governor of Tennessee (the large gravestone was placed there by the state a century after his death).

WESTON FULTON MEMORIAL, HIGHLAND CEMETERY

WESTON FULTON *invented a device that enabled* DEPTH CHARGES *and* AIR CONDITIONERS

KNOXVILLE HISTORY GUIDE SPONSORS

The Board of Directors and the staff of the Knoxville History Project deeply appreciate the support and generosity of our sponsors to underwrite the cost of production for the first edition of this historical and cultural guide.

Without your support, this book would not have been possible.

PILOT FLYING J

VISIT KNOXVILLE

DAUGHTERS OF THE AMERICAN REVOLUTION, EMORY ROAD CHAPTER

IN ADDITION, SUPPORT WAS PROVIDED BY JOE SULLIVAN, AND CITY OF KNOXVILLE COUNCIL MEMBERS: FINBARR SAUNDERS, MARSHALL STAIR, AND DUANE GRIEVE.

Sponsor Statement

Pilot Flying J is proud to be headquartered in Knoxville, Tennessee, since 1958.

When James A. Haslam II, a 1952 University of Tennessee graduate and starting tackle on the 1951 national championship football team, founded Pilot Corporation, it was a family-owned business with one gas station. Today, the company has grown to become Pilot Flying J, the nation's largest operator of travel centers in North America.

Pilot Flying J operates a network of more than 750 travel centers and employs more than 26,000 team members, connecting people and places with comfort, care and a smile at every stop. CEO Jimmy Haslam, son of founder Jim Haslam, led Pilot Flying J's growth to serve 1.3 million guests daily by 2018, the year of the company's 60th anniversary.

Pilot Flying J's legacy is rooted in Knoxville, and the Tennessee "volunteer spirit" is engrained in its culture. With a long history of giving back, Pilot Flying J's philanthropy continues today across the country, focusing on education and youth development, safety, wellness and veterans. In East Tennessee, the company supports longstanding organizations such as Knoxville History Project, Knoxville Symphony Orchestra, Knoxville Museum of Art, East Tennessee Historical Society, Tennessee Theatre, Lakeshore Park, United Way of Greater Knoxville, Boys & Girls Clubs of the Tennessee Valley and many others.

"To whom much is given, much is required." - JAMES A. HASLAM II

Sponsor Statement

TENNESSEE

———•———

Jack Neely once described Knoxville as "America concentrated in one spot". Appreciated by generations of Knoxville natives, the city's rich and surprising history is also a draw for visitors. From industry to art, music to mountains, culture to cuisine, visitors from around the world find ways to connect to Knoxville. Many of them do so in a personal way, learning about their own history through the premier genealogy research library at the East Tennessee History Center. Others discover it through our museums and galleries. Knoxville's Urban Wilderness also provides insight into the history of the land and our ties to the Great Smoky Mountains National Park. Everywhere you turn, there's a reflection of the past in what is presented in today's vibrant landscape.

As the official Convention and Visitors Bureau for the city of Knoxville and Knox County, Visit Knoxville promotes the history and culture of Knoxville every day. We send (and accompany) guests to historic sites, museums and galleries and collaborate with those organizations to share the stories of our heritage.

Visit Knoxville is committed to the past, present and future of this city and greatly appreciates the ongoing efforts of the Knoxville History Project. Thank you for preserving and promoting the story of Knoxville.

Sponsor Statement

Throughout the history of National Society Daughters of the American Revolution (DAR) Historic Preservation has always been one of the main focuses of the mission of the organization. DAR members participate in a wide variety of Historic Preservation projects as it is crucial to saving our history for future generations. Some of these projects include: commemorations and memorials, restoring and maintaining historical sites, locating and marking patriot headstones, and preserving genealogical records, artifacts and historical documents.

Through the Special Projects Grants Program, the DAR provides local community grant funding to support projects exemplifying the organization's mission areas of Historic Preservation, Education and Patriotism. In conjunction with the local chapter, Emory Road, we are pleased to provide support to the Knoxville History Project for this Knoxville History Guide.

WRITER and **RESEARCHER** *Jack Neely* is longtime journalist whose award-winning column, "Secret History," appeared in *Metro Pulse* for more than 20 years. He's author of numerous books about Knoxville's distinctive history, including, recently, *The Tennessee Theatre: A Grand Entertainment Palace*, *Market Square: The History of the Most Democratic Place on Earth*, and *Knoxville, Tennessee: This Obscure Prismatic City*. His work has been recognized by the Society of Professional Journalists, the Tennessee Library Association, the American Institute of Architects, and the University of Tennessee's History Department. Since 2014 he has served as executive director of the Knoxville History Project.

EDITOR *Paul James* is director of publishing and development for the Knoxville History Project. From Derby, England, James is the former executive director of Ijams Nature Center and author of books of local history himself, notably his popular book on the unique story of Ijams.

Robin Easter Design is a full-service graphic design firm located in Knoxville's Historic Old City. For nearly 30 years, they have been known for their award-winning custom design and illustration. Art Director and **DESIGNER**, *Whitney Sanders*, gained national recognition for the studio for her design of *The Tennessee Theatre: A Grand Entertainment Palace*.

KNOXVILLE HISTORY PROJECT

THE KNOXVILLE HISTORY PROJECT (KHP) is a private, educational nonprofit organization with a mission to research, preserve, and promote the unique history of Knoxville, a city whose past makes it distinct from all other places. We strive to research and publish new compelling stories and create historical experiences that are memorable, educational, and relevant to the city's future.

KHP provides talks, tours, podcasts, documentaries, and public art. We work with property owners, developers, and government agencies to research historic individuals, events, buildings, and places.

KHP's main source of revenue is philanthropic contributions. Please consider making a donation to support the preservation of Knoxville history for generations to come.

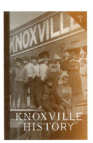    

Make a donation or support our work by purchasing a publication online at **KNOXVILLEHISTORYPROJECT.ORG**

Thank you for your support

BEYOND THE GUIDEBOOK

A NEW WAY OF EXPERIENCING KNOXVILLE HISTORY ONLINE

The Knoxville History Portal is an online repository featuring all facets of Knoxville's history through stories, image galleries, video interviews and documentaries, podcasts, artwork, and more!

GO TO **KNOXVILLEHISTORYPROJECT.ORG/PORTAL**

KNOXVILLE WALKING TOURS

EARLY YEARS
CIVIL WAR
SHADOW SIDE GHOST TOUR
MUSICAL HISTORY

GUNSLINGERS
LITERARY HERITAGE
SHADOW SIDE —
GHOSTS OF THE OLD CITY

Join poet and storyteller Laura Still, author of *A Haunted History Knoxville*, for a historical tour of Downtown Knoxville—its, past, its present, and most of all, its people. Laura opens a window to Knoxville's varied past and leads you on a journey through hard times and high times of a city growing through more than two centuries of history.

"Laura Still was already a published poet before she got into the tour-guide business. She's the one who can tell these stories. She has combined an open mind with real and diligent library research into very specific stories that aren't duplicated in other cities." - **JACK NEELY, KNOXVILLE HISTORY PROJECT**

Tour descriptions, prices, and dates online at **KNOXVILLEWALKINGTOURS.COM**

A portion of all downtown tours support the Knoxville History Project

Acknowledgments

The Knoxville History Project would like to thank the following for their help in producing this book

◆

AKIMA CLUB OF KNOXVILLE
ROBIN EASTER DESIGN
SHAWN POYNTER PHOTOGRAPHY
SAM FURROW FOR SHARING VINTAGE POSTCARDS FROM THE SAM FURROW KNOXVILLE DIGITAL POSTCARD COLLECTION
ADRIENNE WEBSTER FOR SHARING VINTAGE POSTCARDS FROM THE LIB COOPER KNOXVILLE DIGITAL POSTCARD COLLECTION

ADAM ALFREY EAST TENNESSEE HISTORY CENTER ◆ **JULIA BARHAM** FARRAGUT MUSEUM ◆ **COURTNEY BERGMEIER** BIJOU THEATRE ◆ **LINDA BILLMAN** ◆ **REBECCA BRIGGS** UNIVERSITY OF TENNESSEE LIBRARY ◆ **HOLLIE COOK** KNOX HERITAGE ◆ **STEVE COTHAM & SALLY POLHEMUS** CALVIN M. MCCLUNG HISTORICAL COLLECTION, KNOX COUNTY PUBLIC LIBRARY ◆ **ERIC DAWSON** TENNESSEE ARCHIVE FOR MOVING IMAGE AND SOUND, KNOX COUNTY PUBLIC LIBRARY ◆ **BOB DAVIS** ◆ **DAVID DOTSON** DOLLYWOOD FOUNDATION ◆ **BECKY HANCOCK** TENNESSEE THEATRE ◆ **DAVE HEARNES** BLOUNT MANSION ◆ **CHEREL HENDERSON** EAST TENNESSEE HISTORICAL SOCIETY ◆ **RUTH REMMERS** GIRL SCOUTS OF THE SOUTHERN APPALACHIANS ◆ **NELDA HILL** KNOX COUNTY PUBLIC LIBRARY ◆ **PATRICK HOLLIS** MABRY HAZEN HOUSE ◆ **JEFF JOHNSON** ◆ **RENEÉ KESLER** BECK CULTURAL EXCHANGE CENTER ◆ **JOHN GAMMON** MARBLE SPRINGS ◆ **JUDY LAROSE** RAMSEY HOUSE ◆ **SAM MAYNARD** JAMES WHITE'S FORT ◆ **JUDY MCMILLAN** CRESCENT BEND ◆ **ROBERT MCGINNIS** JAMES WHITE'S FORT ◆ **DEBBIE WILSON** BLEAK HOUSE ◆ **LAURA ROMANS** UNIVERSITY OF TENNESSEE LIBRARY ◆ **NICKI RUSSLER** ◆ **TOM SCHIRTZ** MCCLUNG MUSEUM OF NATURAL HISTORY AND CULTURE ◆ **CAT SHTEYNBERG** MCCLUNG MUSEUM OF NATURAL HISTORY AND CULTURE ◆ **ALAN SIMS** INSIDEOFKNOXVILLE.COM ◆ **ANGELA THOMAS** KNOXVILLE MUSEUM OF ART ◆ **DEBBIE SHAW** TENNESSEE STATE MUSEUM ◆ **MEGAN SPAINHOUR** TENNESSEE STATE LIBRARY & ARCHIVES ◆ **MARY WORKMAN** ◆ **MEREDITH JAMES** ◆ **ISABEL JAMES**

Photo Credits

**NELS AKERLUND /
TENNESSEE THEATRE**
53

**BECK CULTURAL
EXCHANGE CENTER**
123 • 124 *bottom*
149 *top*

BLOUNT MANSION
5 *left* • 24

BRUCE COLE
18 *right* • 127 *bottom*

**LIB COOPER
DIGITAL KNOXVILLE
POSTCARD COLLECTION**
14 *left* • 135 *top*

CRESCENT BEND
28 *top* • 29

**ESTATE OF BEAUFORD
DELANEY, BY
PERMISSION OF DEREK
L. SPRATLEY, ESQUIRE,
COURT APPOINTED
ADMINISTRATOR**
39 *center right*

DOLLYWOOD FOUNDATION
87 *center right*

**EAST TENNESSEE
HISTORICAL SOCIETY
(ETHS)**
56 *bottom*

ELIZABETH FELICELLA
144 *bottom*

**SAM FURROW KNOXVILLE
POSTCARD COLLECTION**
17 • 36 *bottom*
68 *bottom* • 84
86 *top* • 105 *bottom*
107 *top* • 119 *bottom*
145 *bottom* • 155 *top*

**JEFF GOLDBERG / ESTO
UT COLLEGE OF
ARCHITECTURE + DESIGN**
108

**CALVIN M. MCCLUNG
HISTORICAL COLLECTION
(CMMHC)**
4 • 6 • 9 • 10
11 *left* • 47 *bottom*
55 • 57 • 61 • 62
71 • 76 *top*
82 *bottom left*
111 *left* • 117 *top*
118 • 121 • 125 *top*
132 *left* • 139 *top*
146 *bottom*
148 *top* • 150 *bottom*
151 *bottom*
152 *bottom*
157 *bottom* • 158

SHARON HANLEY / ETHS
31 *left*

**IJAMS FAMILY
COLLECTION**
154 *bottom*

IJAMS NATURE CENTER
154 *top*

ISABEL JAMES
130 *bottom*

**KNOX COUNTY TWO
CENTURIES PHOTOGRAPH
PROJECT, CMMHC**
139 *top*

**KNOXVILLE
BOTANICAL GARDEN**
142

**KNOXVILLE
HISTORY PROJECT**
5 *right* • 13 *left*
15 • 23 *left*

**KNOXVILLE MUSEUM
OF ART**
39 *left, right top &
bottom* • 132 *bottom*

LIBRARY OF CONGRESS
2 *bottom* • 11 *right*
13 *right* • 66 • 88
90 • 92 • 93 *top*
119 *top* • 129 *top left*
141 *top* • 165 • 182

MABRY-HAZEN HOUSE
32 *left*

MARBLE SPRINGS
26 *top* • 27 *right*

**MCCARTY HOLSAPLE
MCCARTY**
41 *top*

**MCCLUNG MUSEUM
OF NATURAL HISTORY
AND CULTURE**
40

ROSS MOL
16 *right*

MIKE O'NEIL
34 • 35

SHAWN POYNTER
2 *top* • 19 *top* • 44
63 • 65 • 67 *top*
68 *top* • 72
81 *bottom* • 97 *bottom*
98 *top* • 112 • 114
116 *left* • 117 *bottom*
134 *top* • 136
153 • 160
162 *bottom*
177 *bottom* • 185

RAMSEY HOUSE
22 *bottom*

**RUSSELL FAMILY /
TOWN OF FARRAGUT**
140 *top* • 141 *bottom*

**ROBIN EASTER DESIGN
ERIK VASS**
1 • 51 *top*
60 *bottom* • 64 *bottom*
68 *top* • 70
94 *right & bottom*
95 *top* • 99 *left*
103 *top*

**MARY U. ROTHROCK
PAPERS**
4

JOHN SANDERS
127 *top*

**ALAN SIMS,
INSIDEOFKNOXVILLE.COM**
19 *bottom* • 75 • 77

TAMIS
85 • 86 *bottom*
87 *left top & left bottom*
138 *right*
172 *left bottom*

**TENNESSEE STATE
LIBRARY & ARCHIVES**
46 *top*

**TENNESSEE STATE
MUSEUM**
7

**THOMPSON PHOTOGRAPH
COLLECTION, CMMHC**
9 • 52 • 106 *bottom*

THREE RIVERS RAMBLER
69 *right*

TOWN OF FARRAGUT
42 *top* • 91

**UNIVERSITY OF
TENNESSEE ATHLETICS**
16 *left*

**UT LIBRARY, SPECIAL
COLLECTIONS**
8 • 12 • 50 • 100
109 • 132 *right*

JIM WEST
163 *top*

MARY WORKMAN
58

*all remaining
photographs by*
PAUL JAMES
for KHP

Map Key

HISTORIC HOMES

1. JAMES WHITE'S FORT — 20
2. RAMSEY HOUSE — 23
3. BLOUNT MANSION — 24
4. MARBLE SPRINGS — 26
5. CRESCENT BEND — 28
6. BLEAK HOUSE — 31
7. MABRY-HAZEN HOUSE — 32
8. WESTWOOD — 34

MUSEUMS & COLLECTIONS

1. EAST TENNESSEE HISTORY CENTER — 37
2. BECK CULTURAL EXCHANGE CENTER — 38
3. KNOXVILLE MUSEUM OF ART — 39
4. MCCLUNG MUSEUM — 40
5. JOHN C. HODGES LIBRARY — 41
6. FARRAGUT MUSEUM — 42
7. WOMEN'S BASKETBALL HALL OF FAME — 42
8. GIRL SCOUT MUSEUM — 43
9. KNOX COUNTY MUSEUM OF EDUCATION — 43
10. ARNSTEIN JEWISH COMMUNITY CENTER — 43

DOWNTOWN

1. OLD COURTHOUSE — 45
2. POST OFFICE — 47
3. MEDICAL ARTS BUILDING — 48
4. JAMES PARK HOUSE — 48
5. LAWSON MCGHEE LIBRARY — 48
6. YMCA — 48
7. YWCA — 48
8. BIJOU THEATRE & LAMAR HOUSE — 50
9. TENNESSEE THEATRE — 53
10. ANDREW JOHNSON HOTEL — 54
11. PLAZA TOWER — 54
12. JOURNAL ARCADE BUILDING — 54
13. FARRAGUT HOTEL — 55
14. MECHANICS BANK & TRUST BUILDING — 56
15. MILLER'S DEPARTMENT STORE — 56
16. TAILOR LOFTS BUILDING — 56
17. CENTURY BUILDING — 56
18. PHOENIX BUILDING — 56
1. EAST TENNESSEE HISTORY CENTER — 59
19. HOLSTON BUILDING — 59
20. S&W CAFETERIA — 59
21. REBORI BUILDING — 60
22. STERCHI BUILDING — 60
23. CAL JOHNSON BUILDING — 61
24. PETER KERN BUILDING — 63
25. PEMBROKE BUILDING — 64
26. DAYLIGHT BUILDING — 64
27. MASONIC TEMPLE — 64
28. PATRICK SULLIVAN'S SALOON — 66
29. BOYD'S JIG & REEL BUILDING — 66
30. RICHARDSONIAN ROMANESQUE BUILDINGS — 67
31. JFG FLATS — 67
32. WHITE LILY FLATS — 68
33. SOUTHERN RAILWAY STATION — 69
34. KNOXVILLE HIGH SCHOOL — 70
35. GALLOWS HILL — 70

DOWNTOWN CHURCHES

1. FIRST PRESBYTERIAN — 73
2. FIRST BAPTIST — 73
3. ST. JOHN'S EPISCOPAL — 74
4. CHURCH STREET METHODIST — 75
5. IMMACULATE CONCEPTION — 76
6. ST. JOHN'S LUTHERAN CHURCH — 76

STATUES

1. STATUE OF A FIREMAN — 78
2. THE DOUGHBOY — 79
3. SPANISH-AMERICAN WAR STATUE — 79
4. VIETNAM MEMORIAL — 79
5. THE OARSMAN — 79
6. ALEX HALEY — 79
7. BELOVED WOMAN OF JUSTICE — 80
8. SERGEI RACHMANINOFF — 80
9. ROTARY CLUB CENTENNIAL STATUE — 80
10. WOMAN SUFFRAGE MEMORIAL — 80
11. FEBB & HARRY BURN — 80
12. THE VOLUNTEER — 81
13. EUROPA & THE BULL — 81
14. GEN. ROBERT NEYLAND — 81
15. PAT SUMMITT — 81
16. LINCOLN: THE FINAL SUMMATION — 81
17. ADMIRAL FARRAGUT — 81
18. TREATY OF THE HOLSTON — 81

THE CIVIL WAR

1	BATTLE OF CAMPBELL'S STATION	90
2	BATTLE OF FORT SANDERS	91
8	LAMAR HOUSE	92
3	DEAF & DUMB ASYLUM	93
4	AVERY RUSSELL HOUSE	93
5	KENNEDY-BAKER HOUSE	94
6	BAKER-PETERS HOUSE	94
7	STATESVIEW	94
8	KNOLLWOOD	95
6	BLEAK HOUSE	95
5	CRESCENT BEND	95
7	MABRY-HAZEN HOUSE	95
G	BETHEL CEMETERY	96
9	FORT STANLEY	96
10	FORT DICKERSON	96
11	FORT HIGLEY	97
C	NATIONAL CEMETERY	98
B	OLD GRAY	98

UNIVERSITY OF TENNESSEE

1	THE HILL	101
2	AYRES HALL	102
3	SOUTH COLLEGE	103
4	AUSTIN PEAY	103
5	ALUMNI MEMORIAL HALL	104
6	HOSKINS LIBRARY	104
7	CIRCLE PARK	105
8	NEYLAND STADIUM	106
9	THOMPSON BOLING ARENA	107
10	ART + ARCHITECTURE BUILDING	108
11	NATALIE HASLAM MUSIC CENTER	108
12	CAROUSEL THEATRE	108
13	CLARENCE BROWN THEATRE	109
14	MCCLUNG PLAZA	110
5	HODGES LIBRARY	110
15	BAKER CENTER FOR PUBLIC POLICY	110
16	TYSON ALUMNI HOUSE	111
17	HOPECOTE	112
18	MORGAN HALL	112
19	UT GARDENS	112
20	WAR DOG MEMORIAL	112
21	UT'S INDIAN MOUND	112
★	VISITOR CENTER	60
🚂	THREE RIVERS RAMBLER	69
--	LIFESAVER WALK	84
....	CATFISH WALK	84

PARKS & GARDENS

A	KRUTCH PARK	143
B	WORLD'S FAIR PARK	143
C	EMORY PLACE	146
D	FOUNTAIN CITY PARK	146
E	RACHEFF GARDENS	147
F	SHARPS RIDGE	148
G	CAL JOHNSON PARK	148
H	ALEX HALEY HERITAGE SQUARE	149
I	CASWELL PARK	149
J	KNOXVILLE BOTANICAL GARDEN	150
K	CHILHOWEE PARK	151
L	ZOO KNOXVILLE	152
M	HOLSTON RIVER PARK	152
10	FORT DICKERSON PARK	153
11	HIGH GROUND PARK / FORT HIGLEY	153
N	IJAMS NATURE CENTER	154
O	SUTTREE LANDING PARK	155
P	MARY VESTAL PARK	155
Q	JAMES AGEE PARK	156
7	CIRCLE PARK	156
R	LAKESHORE PARK	156
S	SEQUOYAH HILLS PARK	158
T	TYSON PARK	158
U	THIRD CREEK GREENWAY	158
V	WEST HILLS / JOHN BYNON PARK	159

CEMETERIES

A	FIRST PRESBYTERIAN GRAVEYARD	161
B	OLD GRAY	163
C	NATIONAL CEMETERY	164
D	LYNNHURST CEMETERY	166
E	GREENWOOD CEMETERY	166
F	CALVARY CEMETERY	167
G	BETHEL CEMETERY	167
H	POTTERS FIELD CEMETERY	168
I	ODD FELLOWS CEMETERY	168
J	OLD JEWISH CEMETERY	168
K	LEBANON-IN-THE-FORKS CEMETERY	169
L	ASBURY CEMETERY	169
M	WOODLAWN CEMETERY	170
N	ISLAND HOME BAPTIST CHURCH	170
O	MOUNT OLIVE CEMETERY	170
P	NEW JEWISH CEMETERY	171
Q	WEST VIEW CEMETERIES	171
R	NEW GRAY CEMETERY	172
S	HIGHLAND MEMORIAL	172